Wicked
GEORGETOWN

Wicked GEORGETOWN

Scoundrels, Sinners and Spies

....

Canden Schwantes

Charleston · London

THE
History
PRESS

Published by The History Press
Charleston, SC 29403
www.historypress.net

Copyright © 2013 by Canden Schwantes
All rights reserved

First published 2013

Manufactured in the United States

ISBN 978.1.62619.005.4

Library of Congress CIP data applied for.

Contents

Acknowledgements

Since I'm writing this section before I've actually finished writing the book, some of these are pre-emptive thank-yous for the stress I knew I'd put you through! None of my research, writing or long days would be possible without the support of my partner, Manny. My mom and dad have already read this book a few times from rough draft to final, so if there are any spelling errors, you can blame them. A special thanks to Ballad've (Margaret and Anders) for serenading my writing sessions and the owners of Jacob's Coffee House for serving me endless cups of tea. None of this would have been possible without Hannah and everyone at The History Press, my colleagues at DC By Foot and the DC Historical Society and Kiplinger Research Library. And a special thanks to you for being interested in the darker side of Georgetown!

Chapter 1

The Less Scandalous Georgetown

A Background

E very neighborhood has skeletons in its closet—even those with the "best addresses" known for being home to the rich and famous, celebrities and senators. Well, maybe we should've expected it from the senators. Georgetown's closets may be walk-ins, but they still have their share of secrets and well-dressed skeletons. From nuns who ran away from the convent to spying for the enemy during the Civil War, the Georgetown rumor mill had plenty of fodder to keep itself running.

Georgetown is a neighborhood, but mention the name to someone unfamiliar with the area and they will likely think of the university. This enclave of elites is more than a habitat of academics and researchers. Today, Georgetown has the reputation of being a high-society neighborhood, but that wasn't always the case. The small town begin in 1751 as a port along the Potomac River, and it was probably not named after the George you are thinking of. You were thinking of George Clooney, weren't you? Although there is not an agreement on the namesake, it's likely named for either George II, King of England at the time when Maryland was still a colony, or after the two landowners from whom the land was bought: George Gordan and George Beall.

There were multiple landowners in the area when the Maryland General Assembly decided to form a town along Rock Creek and the Potomac River. These land holdings had interesting names such as Conjurer's

Georgetown University's Healy Hall. *Library of Congress.*

Disappointment, Resurvey on Salp, Frogland and Pretty Prospect. But the holdings that were chosen to become George Town were the tracts Knave's Disappointment, Beall's Level and Rock of Dumbarton. George Beall was very much against the purchasing of his land, but the Maryland Assembly was not so much offering to purchase it as it was telling him he had to sell. He reluctantly agreed to the purchase price but included a letter protesting the

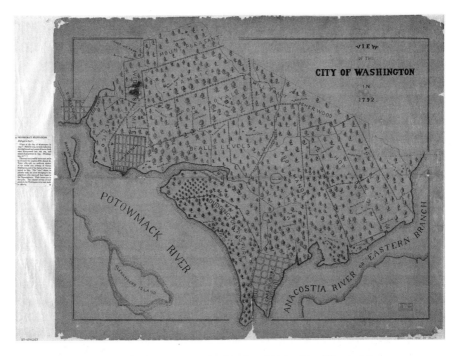

A 1792 map showing what would become the District of Columbia. *Library of Congress.*

acts and preserving his right to seek future redress. In addition to payment for their lands, each George got to pick two lots in the new town.

The city thrived along the Potomac River as a tobacco inspection station and continued to grow through the years. Traders and merchants began to move to the area from the nearby farms. One of these men was Christopher Lehman, a German immigrant living in Pennsylvania who wished to trade the farm life for a profession in woodworking. He moved to Georgetown and was able to purchase land on the main street and began building a house of stone. The Old Stone House, as it is called today, was built in 1765 and is the oldest structure in the area still standing.

Georgetown proved an ideal location for business meetings and lodgings once the United States government decided to move the capital from New York City to a new location. Congress agreed to locate the new federal district in the undeveloped area along the Potomac River between the Eastern Branch (now called the Anacostia River) and the Connogocheque Creek with lands from both Maryland and Virginia. At this point, there was not much there other than swamplands and farms and a few small clusters of buildings that could *maybe* be called villages. But there *was* Georgetown.

Old postcard of Georgetown. *Library of Congress.*

Georgetown had roads to drive on, inns to stay at, taverns to drink in and the rich men needed to fund the whole endeavor. It was here that George Washington met with these wealthy residents to discuss the speculation of soon-to-be federal lands. The District of Columbia was to be one hundred square miles and include the port cities of Georgetown and Alexandria.

According to legend, Georgetown may have played a part in the layout of the federal city, including where its main attraction, the Capitol, is located. Washington's city planner, Peter (Pierre) Charles L'Enfant was to set out and view for himself the landscape of the area to envision his plan. With Congress paying off a war, there was not much in the coffers to build a new city from scratch, and President Washington was mostly on his own in figuring out how to pay for it. His idea was to have investors purchase plots of land in anticipation of selling them for a profit once the city was completed. With the location of the city to be in the general area between Georgetown and the village of Carrollsburgh, Washington decided to pit these towns against one another. Should the wealthy residents of Georgetown see L'Enfant showing an interest closer to Carrollsburgh, they might offer to pay more for the plots of land closer to their homes.

Of course, the plan backfired. As L'Enfant wandered closer to Carrollsburgh near the Anacostia River, he came across Jenkin's Hill, declaring it "a pedestal awaiting a superstructure." He decided that this was the perfect place for the people's part of the government—the Congress House. Thomas Jefferson later dubbed it the Capitol, paying homage to the Rome's Capitoline Hill. Jenkin's Hill was much closer to Carrollsburgh than Georgetown, but L'Enfant was not concerned about this. If he had more of a financial stake or, rather, had he cared more about the financial stake in this endeavor, the Capitol building and center of D.C. might be a bit closer to Georgetown.

Though today Washington and D.C. are interchangeable, it wasn't always so. D.C. included the separate municipalities of Washington, Georgetown, Alexandria, Washington Country and Alexandria County. Georgetown continued to develop on its own until 1871, when its governmental powers were revoked and it officially became nothing more politically than a neighborhood in the District.

There are still remnants of Georgetown being a separate city before D.C. enveloped it. To match the lettered and numbered streets of the city, Georgetown's roads were renamed. What used to be called Bridge Street became M Street NW, the main thoroughfare of the area. But not all of the lettered streets match up as they cross over Wisconsin Ave NW, formally High Street. They weren't planned to continue along as one road.

The location of the city of Georgetown had much to do with the Potomac River, as did the location of the capital city. In the early 1800s, the Georgetown

Georgetown street scene. *Author's collection.*

Drawing by Susan Chase Brown of Old Georgetown, D.C. *Library of Congress.*

part of the Potomac wasn't navigable thanks to tidal changes bringing in more and more silt. To correct this issue, the Chesapeake and Ohio (C&O) Canal was built. This more navigable waterway connected Georgetown to Cumberland, Maryland. The C&O Canal, known as the Grand Ole Ditch, was never profitable for the company due to competition with the Baltimore and Ohio Railroad, but it did bring much needed business into Georgetown.

When the C&O Canal began to falter both economically and physically, Georgetown's industry failed. With no passable waterway, shipping in the area floundered. But the waterfront area remained industrious and was home to a flourmill, meat-rendering plant, lumberyard and the Capital Traction Company power plant. The industrious part of the neighborhood close to the waterfront continues today as retail outlets.

With business moving away from Georgetown, there was a time that the homes built for the rich and famous were lived in by the poor and unknown. As the merchants and traders left, many free blacks moved into the area.

Without the means and economic ability to rebuild or alter the homes, they remained as they were.

The closets these Georgetown skeletons are kept in aren't always closets at all but the semi-liveable spaces for the slaves of Georgetown. Georgetown was a port city after all, and as the tobacco trade floundered, the slave trade flourished. The slaves and free blacks living in the area were not accorded any special privileges living in the capital of the Union. They were not allowed to congregate in public places, with the exception of church. The exterior staircase on the side of St. John's the Divine in Georgetown remains today as a reminder of the strict separation of the two races.

Slave trading began in Georgetown in the 1790s, when John Beattie established his business there. McCandless Tavern, in the center of the neighborhood's busiest intersection, had a slave pen for slaves waiting to be sold. After the Emancipation Act, the newly freed slaves, including those coming from the seceded southern states, started moving to Georgetown. The ups and downs of Georgetown gentrification began with the movement of these freed slaves. Eventually, the population of blacks nearly doubled, with both a professional and working class. They continued the tradition of congregating in churches, and many historically black churches are still worshipping in Georgetown today, though their congregations tend to be bussed in from other areas.

This dingy, industrial town with an established black community was the Georgetown of the late nineteenth century. But then the industries moved, the canal closed and the Great Depression hit. Blacks were not allowed to ~~take the public transport into the city~~ to work for the government's New Deal project.[1] After World War II, the boom of governmental jobs brought in waves of new young professionals looking for affordable housing. They found it in Georgetown. These young professionals continued the revitalization of the poorer industrial area throughout the decades. In the 1960s, a well-established young congressman from a historically political family moved down the street. John F. Kennedy lived here as both senator and president, and his wife, Jackie, lived here after his assassination.

The Kennedys are often credited with bringing Georgetown to the forefront of high society. Perhaps they added their influence to the redevelopment of Georgetown's reputation, but it was a preferred place to live well before the Kennedys moved in. Throughout history, the homes of wealthy merchants, influential government officials and society women have dotted the Georgetown landscape.

1. Not true. They were allowed to take public transport.

John F. and Jackie Kennedy's pre–White House home on N Street NW. *Author's collection.*

Today, Georgetown does a good job of protecting its reputation. After a walk through the hills among historic homes, viewing mansions through the ancient trees, you'll see why so many people want to live there. The neighborhood of Georgetown is older than both the city and the "state" in which it is located. It holds the footprints of some of the most influential persons in the country's founding and continued development. Sometimes, these tracks were not covered as well as they thought and we can trace them back through the scandalous side of Georgetown.

Chapter 2

Secesh Spies in a Union Town

Washington, D.C., was the capital of the Union during the Civil War, but that doesn't mean that everyone living there was a supporter. In many ways, the district was an isolated bubble of Union support. Just across the Potomac River was the Confederate state of Virginia, and just beyond the northern district line was the nearly secessionist state of Maryland. Even within the district itself, there were many families with Southern sympathies. They were referred to as "secesh families," and Georgetown had quite a few.

It was a touchy thing to live in Washington, D.C., and keep your alliances with the enemy. Not everyone was so adept at keeping their feelings to themselves. With the battles raging just over the bridge, much of the capital city was turned into training grounds, barracks and hospitals. Miss English's Seminary For Young Ladies in Georgetown was the school of many daughters of the elite. There the young girls would be educated on "that amount of mental and moral culture necessary to render them amiable, intelligent, and useful members of society," as stated in the school's brochure. Since Miss Lydia English was an amiable and useful member of society, her home was turned into a Union hospital during the Civil War. And as she was an intelligent lady (despite the fact that she was a staunch supporter of the Southern states), rather than publically object to the intrusion, she simply moved around the corner, where she did not have to see that Union flag flying on her former home. The doctor brought into treat in the Union

Union soldiers in front of Miss Lydia English's seminary during its Civil War Union hospital days. *Library of Congress.*

soldiers, Dr. Armistead Peter, was also a Southern sympathizer, but he treated the men nonetheless.

Many families in Georgetown very much supported the Union and were pleased to offer their assistance. Samuel Hein hung a Union flag in his window every day for the entirety of the war, and he offered what aid he could to the wounded and battle-weary Union troops returning to D.C. through Georgetown after the bloody battles in Virginia. For two days after the Battle of Manassas, Hein used his backyard to offer returning soldiers food on their way through.

A GOOD SOUTHERN SON

Georgetown families that did not agree with Mr. Hein not only secretly sided with the Confederacy—they sometimes supported it outright and sent their sons across the lines. The Wheatley family lived on N Street NW, where their home still stands. Charles and Francis Wheatley had joined the Confederate Army of Northern Virginia under the command of Robert E. Lee. In 1865, their younger brother Walter saved what he could to purchase the necessities for war—pipes, tobacco and a bit of courage—and then made his way across the lines to join Mosby's command. He hadn't been there long before his brother Francis was killed in battle. Being a good Southern son, rather than let his mother hear of this news from strangers on the doorstep, he decided to return home himself. Walter was able to retrieve from Francis's belongings a pocket watch and a photograph.

Walter appeared to the delight of most of the household. However, not everyone in the Wheatley household was pleased to see his return. One of the slaves informed a Union official of the presence of a Confederate spy. Actual intent to gather military intelligence was not necessary for young Walter to be hanged as a spy; his mere presence would suffice. Fearing for his life, Walter ran to hide when he heard the soldiers coming. As he left his room, he came upon a large water tank and crawled inside. But the same slave who revealed his presence also revealed his hiding place.

The German mercenaries hired to patrol Georgetown began to stab their bayonets into the water tank. Rather than be killed in hiding as a spy, the dripping wet Walter Wheatley came out of the water tank and was arrested on the spot. He was held in the Old Capitol Prison for a short period of time. The Wheatley family had some social and political influence, and with the war nearly over, they were able to arrange Walter's release.

Not all those found to be Confederate spies were so lucky. Despite a strong relationship with many in power, William O. Williams and Gip Peter discovered what happened when charged as a Confederate spy. On the morning of June 9, 1863, at Fort Granger under the command of Union Colonel John Baird, these two Confederate soldiers from one of Georgetown's most prominent families were hanged. They had not succeeded in their mission, if it was indeed a secret mission at all.

"YOU'VE PLAYED THIS DAMNED WELL"

William Orton Williams and Walter Gibson "Gip" Peter were cousins and as part of the Peter family were descendants of George Washington's step-granddaughter. They both grew up at Tudor Place in Georgetown, home

Tudor Place, the family home of Gip Peter and William O. Williams. *Library of Congress.*

of the Peter family from its completion in 1816 to the death of the last owner in 1983. William's mother, America Peter, was one of the three sisters born in Tudor Place to a seemingly patriotic family. The sisters were named America, Columbia and Britannia. But the patriotism to the United States as a whole did not extend past the naming of children. As many of the families in Georgetown, the Peters had Southern sympathies. Their relatives, the Lee family of Virginia, only encouraged this support.

Williams was only a young boy when both his parents passed away. Afterward, he moved to live with relatives at Arlington House (what is now Arlington National Cemetery) and Tudor Place. The owner of Arlington House was George Washington Parke Custis, Robert E. Lee's father-in-law. In one of many acts of nepotism in the military at the time, Lee petitioned to have Williams commissioned in the United States Army. As a second lieutenant in Lee's Second Calvary, Williams was assigned as General Winfield Scott's personal secretary.

In 1861, as the Southern states started to secede, so too did Robert E. Lee and William Orton Williams. But General Scott did not accept the resignation of his personal secretary immediately. With fear that he might

20

have some knowledge that could benefit the Confederate army, Williams was imprisoned for several weeks.

Williams did not have the greatest reputation. He was seen as an arrogant man. After all, he had acquired his position due to family connections and not because of any education or skill on his part. He was also known for once killing a soldier who refused his orders. But despite his inability to get along with his fellow soldiers, he did well in the Confederacy. An official name change to Lawrence Orton Williams and a transfer provided him with a fresh start, as did the arrival of his cousin Gip, who had been a scout in Virginia but put in for a transfer at Williams's request. Colonel Williams, now in command of the Second Brigade of Major General Martin's cavalry, had his cousin at his side and fortune on his side.

Around this same time, Union officers Colonel Lawrence W. Auton and Major George Dunlop were given orders to inspect the Union outposts in the Cumberland and Ohio areas. While traveling along the road with their orderly and possessions, they came across some enemy soldiers. Running for their lives and without a thought of what might be lost in the scuffle other than their heads, Auton and Dunlop escaped at the cost of losing their belongings.

When the soldiers arrived at Fort Granger, they used signed orders from General William Rosecrans and the War Department to gain an audience with Colonel Baird. There was some suspicion due to their civilian overcoats and outdated headwear, but Baird could find little reason to doubt their story and readily assisted where he could. Auton had requested passes that would allow them to continue on to Nashville as soon as possible, as well as a $100 loan to assist in the journey. The other officers at the fort put little faith in the visitors' story, but Baird did not accept their concerns. Many refused to contribute to the loan, and in the end, Baird only had $50 to offer. As the evening waned, Auton and Dunlop said their thanks and goodbyes and rode off on their way to Nashville. At least this was the assumption of Colonel Baird. After they left, Baird realized that he had never seen them inspect the outpost at all. If that was their only reason for being in the area, why had they not taken a look around the fortifications? Later reports from other men at the post state that they did indeed perform a detailed and thorough walkthrough.

Baird, previously an attorney, had been in the military for less than a year. With little formal military training, his actions were not always supported by his men. Though Baird believed the inspectors, few others did. When lifelong soldier Colonel Louis Watkins arrived shortly afterward, Baird related the evening's happenings to seek out his opinion. Watkins thought it best to gain more information and rode out to find the two men. We have no way of knowing how Watkins coerced Auton and Dunlop to return to the fort. The two inspectors were not returned by force, and it is likely that they had been asked to collect some dispatches to bring with them on their way to Nashville.

Upon returning to the fort, it was not dispatches they found but an armed guard. The inspectors persisted with their story but could not offer proof. The proof would be found through communication with Rosecrans to verify the identity of the men and their orders. Fog prevented the signal stations as an option, and the telegram sent to Murfreesboro was not deemed a priority. Fort Granger waited nearly three hours to receive a reply that there had been no such men to his knowledge.

But the questions of veracity could have been answered without the long-awaited telegram. The orders from Rosecrans, signed by James A. Garfield, wrongly identified Garfield's position as assistant adjutant rather than chief of staff. The orders from the War Department were penned on regular stationary with no official letterhead. While Baird had noticed the oddities of their uniforms, he did not see that Auton wore the wrong shoulder boards for an officer staffed by the War Department. However, the orders did state that Auton was a cavalryman, and this could have explained Auton's uniform. The two men arrived through enemy territory with no armed escort and still were able to escape. It was not likely they were who they said they were.

With further interrogation, the two men admitted the farce but denied being spies. Colonel Lawrence W. Auton was indeed a colonel in the Confederate army named Lawrence Orton Williams. Traveling with him was Lieutenant Walter Gibson Peter. But they were not on a mission to retrieve privileged information about the fort or its officers; they were acting on a bet made with fellow Confederate officers that they could eat with and borrow money from the fort's commander.

For a short time, they had won the bet. But in the end, it cost them their lives. With orders from above to call a drumhead court-martial tribunal, Baird was forced to do just that. During times of war, trials were more often than not just for show. There is no innocent until proven guilty, and a set punishment is determined by the crime, regardless of extenuating circumstances. It took less than one hour for the tribunal to declare the men guilty of spying. Watkins eventually recognized Williams. They had served together in the U.S. Army before the war. Watkins and Baird attempted to intervene on the spies' behalf, but it was nearly 4:00 a.m, and Rosecrans and Garfield had gone to bed with direct orders not to be disturbed.

Hanging at Fort Granger of William O. Williams and Gip Peter. Harper's Weekly, *July 4, 1863.*

Williams and Peter handled their sentences with dignity and grace. In his statement during the trial, Williams admitted that he knew the consequences of being found guilty and was fully prepared to accept them. He did plea for the release of young Peter, but to no avail. They never admitted to being spies, only to a duplicitous manner of gaining entrance. Even in the letters they wrote to their loved ones at home, the two declared their innocence.

A final telegram was sent to Rosecrans. Baird made it known that these men were relatives of General Robert E. Lee and that Williams's father had served with Rosecrans in the Mexican-American War. Three hours after the scheduled time of execution, there was still no reply.

As ordered, the men were hanged. It took them twenty minutes to die. Though all were agreed that it was right to hang men condemned as spies and that the two men had brought the actions unto themselves, it was a difficult event to participate in. Both Baird and Watkins refused to watch. All accounts report of the composure and bravery of Gip Peter and William O. Williams, whose lasts words were, "Let us die like men."

Understandably, the Peter family and the South as a whole were outraged. Confederate president Jefferson Davis even wrote to President Lincoln regarding the event. What little solace that could be brought to the families came when the bodies were reburied in Oak Hill Cemetery in Georgetown.

DUPLICITOUS DAUGHTERS OF THE CONFEDERACY

In support of their Southern brothers, some Georgetown families sent their sons across enemy lines—and some even sent their daughters. There are three female Confederate spies buried in Oak Hill Cemetery in Georgetown: Lillie Mackall, Antonia Ford Willard and Bettie Duvall. These women were not the most active spies during the Civil War (that role is reserved for Rose O'Neil Greenhow), but they did assist Greenhow in her mission to serve the South behind the lines.

Rose had many ladies of the Southern persuasion assist in her clandestine messaging. Apart from her daughter, Little Rose, Lillie Mackall may be called her main assistant. Lillie was not remarkable in looks or personality, and this proved a great asset to someone hoping to eavesdrop around the capital city. Rose was not the most organized or professional of spies, as a thorough search of her house later found the codes to ciphers, remnants of messages and lists of her contacts. After Rose was arrested in her home in August 1861, Lillie arrived at the house. It was Lillie who reminded Rose that there were still dispatches in the house that had not yet been sent and letters still in the library not yet destroyed.

Later that evening, with the guards distracted by the liquor left in the house, Rose and Lillie were able to sneak into the library to grab the letters. Rose was essentially under house arrest and would not be able to leave. It would be too risky for her regular network of spies to collect them. Lillie was already there and snuck the letters into her pocket to send after she left the house.

The loyalty Lillie had to Rose and the Confederate cause was strong enough that she asked to be imprisoned with the other suspected female spies in Rose's house. Lillie continued to save the furtive efforts from Rose's disorganization. A blotter that had been used to clear the excess ink from a previous dispatch was found with the message still visible. It was Lillie who destroyed it.

Rose may not have been very stealthy or careful, but she was a remarkable asset to the Confederacy. Her collection of contacts through the Union

Cipher supplied to Confederate spy Rose O'Neal Greenhow. *North Carolina State Archives.*

government was mostly gathered through the cunning ways of a woman. In the end, being such a good spy was what saved her. Everyone was so afraid of who and what she knew that they refused to prosecute her. Even through captivity she was able to sneak messages across the lines through means that no one ever figured out. At some point, her guards decided that Lillie was her connection to the outside web of spies and ordered the young accomplice to leave. She refused to leave the prison house and her friend but was forced out. Not everyone can say they were kicked out of prison.

While away from Rose, Lillie died from a severe illness. She was only twenty-two years old. Rose was heartbroken at the loss of her friend. Despite her close relationship with Lillie, Rose was not allowed to attend the funeral. Lillie Mackall, a descendent of one of the oldest families in Georgetown, is buried at Oak Hill Cemetery in Georgetown with a number of family members.

Not as large of a part of Rose's life but an essential messenger in the Confederate spy ring was Bettie Duvall. Bettie was a well-known beauty with long, brown, luxurious hair. At the age of sixteen, she had no fear or qualms about enlisting to assist her beloved South. Rose had an urgent message for General Beauregard telling of a surprise attack planned by President Lincoln and General McDowell of the Union Army. She passed it along to Bettie to deliver it in person to a Confederate outpost not far from the city.

Dressed as a sweet young milkmaid, Bettie and her farm cart made their way through Georgetown. The First Massachusetts Infantry was headquartered in Georgetown. This young beauty, with a message that would lead to their defeat at the first Battle of Manassas, rode past their camp unchallenged. Once far enough out of the city, she left behind her country outfit and donned a riding habit. Abandoning her cart, she hopped on a horse and galloped toward General Bonham's headquarters in Fairfax Court House. When Confederate soldiers escorted her to Bonham's tent, he first refused to see her under the assumption that she was a spy for the Union. A spy she was, but not for those damned Yankees!

When finally admitted to his presence, Bettie unpinned the bun in her hair and let down her locks. She took out from behind her tousled hair a small package wrapped in silk that had been tucked away in the knot on top of her head. There the note of a few short words had been hidden.

The note prepared the scattered Southern forces for a surprise attack on the afternoon of July 16. With this knowledge, the Confederacy concentrated their forces and waited for the incoming Union troops at Manassas. When the Union forces crossed Bull Run, the Rebels, led by Jackson and his "stonewall," were ready. The Confederate army owed a debt of gratitude

Studio portrait of Antonia Ford Willard. *Library of Congress.*

to Rose for the warning and to Bettie for the note hidden in her hair. Bettie Duvall and her husband, John Converse Webb, are buried in Oak Hill Cemetery. Not far from them is another Southern woman dedicated to the cause, Antonia Ford Willard.

The Fords were a wealthy family from Fairfax Court House, Virginia, just south of D.C. The closeness of the town to the Union lines led it to be the first captured and held by Union forces for most of the war. But this did not change the dedication of the Southern families living there.

With the town under Union control, it was the Ford home that was chosen to house the higher-ranking officers. Antonia Ford, the twenty-three-year-old brunette beauty educated in writing and English literature, found in this an opportunity to serve the Confederate cause. She used her womanly ways and Southern charm to entice the Union soldiers to brag about the strength of their forces and reveal military secrets in order to impress her. At each turn, she reported what she learned to family friends Brigadier General J.E.B Stuart and Colonel John Mosby.

As a thank-you for her efforts, Stuart honorably named her an aide-de-camp and issued a certificate stating as much. In 1862, an actual aide-de-camp of Union general Irvin McDowell arrived in Fairfax Court House to find a house suitable for his headquarters. Major Joseph Willard chose the Ford home. This provided more information for Antonia to share with Stuart, and she informed him of a charade planned by the Union to use Confederate flags as a lure.

After a few months, McDowell left and Brigadier General Edwin Stoughton arrived in his stead. Rather than stay with the Fords, Stoughton sought shelter elsewhere, but he was much in the company of Antonia. Much to the dismay of his men, Stoughton struck up a friendship with the young girl. Their frequent soirees and horseback outings revealed crucial information that she used to assist Colonel Mosby in a great (but foolish) prank on the Union.

Colonel Mosby had learned from Antonia the position of the Federal troops and where Stoughton was staying within the city. In early March 1863, he and a few dozen men arrived in the disguise of Federal soldiers and made their way into the city, untested for the most part. Mosby gained entrance into the home in which Stoughton was drunkenly sleeping. In a brazen act of defiance, Mosby spanked the Union officer on the rear and claimed him his prisoner.

With the help of a female detective, the Federal government was able to determine the source of Mosby's information as Antonia Ford. She refused to take the oath of allegiance, and her house was searched. Her mock commission as a major in Stuart's Calvary was found hidden under her mattress. Antonia was arrested and brought to Washington to be held at the Old Capitol Prison. Also at the prison, now serving on the staff of the provost marshal, was the same Major Willard who had stayed at the Ford house under McDowell. Willard had had an instant attraction to her years ago, and even now, in the midst of poor food, bedbugs and lice, he was still in love with her. He petitioned for her release and in the meantime brought her presents, declaring his love for her.

In the year of her imprisonment, he never told her that he was married. It was an unhappy marriage, but a legal one nonetheless. It took some time for a divorce to be obtained and for Willard to resign from the military, but in March 1864, the confederate spy Antonia Ford married her Union prison guard Major Willard in Washington D.C. Antonia's response to marrying a Union officer: "I knew I could not revenge myself on the nation, but I was fully capable of tormenting one Yankee to death, so I took the major."

THOMAS CONRAD

Thomas Conrad was a Virginia man, born and raised in Fairfax Court House. (It seems this little town was home to a lot of covert operations during the Civil War!) When the Civil War began, Conrad was a twenty-three-year-old teacher living in Georgetown. Conrad was an educated man and a Methodist preacher. He began his career in education as a principal at the all boys' school, the Georgetown Institute.

Thomas Conrad, Civil War spy. *Courtesy of Archives and Special Collections, Dickinson College, Carlise, PA.*

Like many Virginia men, Conrad seceded along with his state. At the outbreak of the war, he was known for his Southern ideals. He was free to express his secessionist opinions thanks to the protection of clergy. He was known in Georgetown as "The Reverend," but the only preaching he did was to encourage his students to join the Confederate army.

Conrad was an ardent secessionist and a proud Virginian. When General Winfield Scott, also a Virginian, remained in the Union Army, Conrad was outraged. He had plans to assassinate the traitor with a musket but was denied permission by the Confederacy. Instead, he used his position at the school to promote the cause. At the 1862 commencement, students wore secessionist badges and promoted the Southern states. Conrad was even able to convince the U.S. Marine Band to play "Dixie." This got him arrested and sent to the Old Capitol Prison. After his release, he continued to gather information and rabble rouse until the Union government had enough and sent him south.

Conrad joined the Confederate Third Virginia Calvary as a chaplain and a scout for J.E.B. Stuart. His background as a well-learned man advanced him to the Confederate Secret Service in 1864. Conrad was asked to develop a way to transfer the gathered intelligence through the lines. His answer was the "Doctor's Line," which allowed physicians sympathetic to the Confederate cause to serve as couriers through Northern Virginia as they made house calls. Doctors were able to move through the lines much more freely and had plenty of room in their medicine bags for covert messages.

Conrad was an essential asset to the Confederacy through the war as a spy and in his recruitment in early days of the war in Georgetown. In Georgetown's 1860 census, only 142 of its 8,766 residents were originally from Northern states. Thomas Conrad and the others found a good place to begin their clandestine work in the secretly secessionist Georgetown.

Chapter 3

Eye Spy

Secret Agents of the Cold War

The Civil War was fought on American soil with guns and daggers in the mid-nineteenth century. Come the twentieth century, there were two world wars and the military tension between competing powers that followed. Just as there were spies hiding in Georgetown supporting the enemy of the Union during the Civil War, a few not-so-good men were in Georgetown as spies leading up to and during the Cold War.

THE PUMPKIN PROVED IT

Alger Hiss maintained his innocence until his death. A former communist turned informant, Whittaker Chambers denounced Hiss as a Soviet spy. But it was a pumpkin that did him in.

Chambers claimed that the two had been the best of friends while members of the Communist Party, a charge that Hiss, who said that he barely knew the man, vehemently denied. Chambers and his wife, Esther, countered this by describing the three homes that the Hisses lived in while in Georgetown. As friends, they met once a week in these Georgetown residences. In the late 1930s, the Hisses lived at 2905 P Street NW, 1245 Thirtieth Street NW and 3415 Volta Place NW.

Above: FBI agent. *Courtesy of the Federal Bureau of Investigation.*

Left: Alger Hiss testifying on the stand. *Library of Congress*

In order to prove his claims, Chambers produced five rolls of thirty-five-millimeter film that showed classified State Department material that Hiss had supposedly given to him. Hiss was an employee at the State Department, from which Chambers claimed he had stolen documents so his wife could type up copies for the Soviets. Chambers had hidden the rolls inside a hollowed-out pumpkin at his Maryland farm. It took a few tries to figure out which pumpkin in the patch held the film.

Alger Hiss was found guilty of perjury for claiming under oath that he had not known Chambers or given him classified documents. The statute of limitations had expired on his suspected spying, but Hiss was sentenced to ten years in prison.

He Preferred the Borscht

The corner of Dumbarton Place and Wisconsin Avenue NW is now a Five Guys burger joint, but in the 1980s, it was an unpretentious French restaurant. On a Saturday night in November 1985, Au Pied du Cochon was serving dinner to two men—one was a junior CIA agent and the other a KGB defector named Vitaly Yurchenko. During the meal, Yurchenko asked if he would be shot if he left the restaurant. After his safety was assured by the agent, Yurchenko left for the restroom. Should he not return within fifteen to twenty minutes, he said, it would not be the young agent's fault.

He did not return. Some reports say he climbed through the bathroom window and left the restaurant, others that he snuck out the back. He could have easily just walked out the front door. Two days later, the Soviet Embassy called a press conference and informed the State Department that they had Vitaly Yurchenko. The embassy is one and half miles from Au Pied du Cochon up Wisconsin Avenue—an easy walk to make before someone starts looking.

Officials later argued over the fault behind the escape. The act proved an embarrassment to the CIA and the United States. French intelligence officers proceeded to mock the CIA for the screw-up by calling them "stupid Americans." To this, the head of the CIA's French desk replied, "We were doing just fine until we took him to a French restaurant!"

An embarrassed CIA and baffled President Reagan could not explain what had happened. Reagan expressed his confusion by saying, "I think it's

Au Pied du Cochon, the site of Vitaly Yurchenko's escape from the CIA. *Courtesy of Spies of Washington.*

awfully easy for any American to be perplexed by anyone who could live in the United States and would prefer to live in Russia." In fact, we still don't know for sure the true motives behind Yurchenko's actions.

After twenty-five years of service with the KGB in the Soviet Union, Yurchenko, a high-ranking official, disappeared while on assignment in Rome. He had informed his guards he would like to visit the Vatican. He never returned. When he was discovered, he was with the CIA. Some say he met his CIA agent in the Sistine Chapel. He was good at disappearing and then turning up on the other side.

There are a few theories regarding what happened afterward. On August 1, Yurchenko sought political asylum at the U.S. Embassy in Rome and defected from the KGB. While in the United States, he provided information to the CIA about KGB operatives acting as spies within their ranks. He named a former CIA trainee who had been fired due to past drug use as the supplier of information. Edward Lee Howard had been trained as an intelligence officer but shortly after being fired started to give confidential information to the Soviets. Yurchenko also named Ronald Pelton. Pelton was an analyst at the National Security Agency and was aware of an upcoming attempt by the United States to tap underwater sea cables. It was Vitaly

Newspapers of Vitaly Yurchenko outside Au Pied du Cochon. *Courtesy of Spies of Washington.*

Yurchenko who he briefed about Operation Ivy Bells in 1980. Thanks to his information, Pelton was arrested, and Howard was investigated until he escaped to Moscow.

Yurchenko claimed that he had been kidnapped by the CIA and had been forced to come the United States. For three months, he was kept in a safe house in Virginia. He was not a willing participant in revealing KGB secrets. Anything he revealed to the CIA, he claimed, was the result of being drugged. It took those three months for him to find an opportunity to escape his captors.

Still another theory is that Yurchenko genuinely wanted to defect but began to miss the motherland after three months. The CIA reported that he was depressed during his stay. Yurchenko required that his water be boiled before he would drink it and started to have hypochondriac tendencies. His mother had died from stomach cancer, and he had developed an ulcer. With advanced medicine in the United States, Yurchenko would have a better chance for a cure if he defected. But he found no cure here.

To add heartbreak to misery, Yurchenko was in love with the Ukrainian wife of a Soviet secretary. When she moved to Canada, he hoped to convince her to defect with him and come to the United States. The CIA even allowed him a trip to Canada for this purpose, but she rejected him and the offer. No cure, no girlfriend, no home. When the press got a hold of his story of defection, it became clear that the Soviets would find out where he was. Yurchenko had been promised that he could disappear and that news of his involvement would be kept from the public. This promise was broken. Had the Soviets found him they would have killed him. Yurchenko knew this firsthand, having been the one to tell the CIA that a Soviet defector who had disappeared in 1975 had been murdered by the KGB. However, if he returned home on his own accord, he might be forgiven. It had happened earlier that year when Oleg Bitov returned to Moscow on the claim that the British had drugged and captured him.

So maybe it was all part of his plan. The Soviet Union accepted his return, but there were reports that he had been executed by a firing squad in Moscow. The report stated that his family was charged for the bullets, but this 1986 report came from the State Department, which was still embarrassed by Yurchenko's actions. Yurchenko was alive and well in Moscow and was never even jailed.

With Yurchenko's information, the CIA began looking into Pelton and Howard, both of whom no longer worked for the government. The Soviets had exhausted all valuable information these two could provide. With the CIA otherwise engaged, the KGB was free to make use of their most senior intelligence agent: Aldrich Ames.

HIDDEN IN PLAIN SIGHT

Aldrich Ames worked with the CIA on its Soviet counterintelligence work in Washington, D.C. Ames had a drinking problem, alimony to an ex-wife and an expensive girlfriend. It took just one piece of information that even Ames did not consider of much value to earn him $50,000.

By the end of his relationship with the Soviets, Ames had a Jaguar and a half-million-dollar home in Arlington that he paid for in cash. His new wife had more than five hundred pairs of shoes and made daily long-distance calls home to Columbia.

On July 13, 1985, at Chadwick's Bar and Grill at 3205 K Street NW in Georgetown, two men met for lunch. One was Aldrich Ames and the other Viktor Cherkashin. Cherkashin worked at the Soviet Embassy as the chief of counterintelligence. Here at Chadwick's, he accepted the names of CIA agents working in the Soviet Union from Ames.

Through the months, Ames learned new and lucrative information. He could walk into the Soviet Embassy on a regular basis to pass along new names as he met with Cherkashin. The two men met openly, and Ames reported back to the CIA that he was attempting to recruit Cherkashin, though in reality, it was the other way around.

There were still times that Ames needed to pass along covert information without carrying it from the CIA to the embassy directly. At the corner of Thirty-seventh and R Street NW in Georgetown, there used to be an ordinary blue USPS mailbox. There is nothing suspicious about a marked-up mailbox, but if you knew what to look for, you

A USPS mailbox similar to the one Aldrich Ames used as a signal. *Author's collection.*

Aldrich Ames after his arrest. *Courtesy of NACIC.*

might notice a chalk mark on the corner. Ames used this tactic to let his handlers know he needed to meet.

As his information about agents reporting on Soviet actions to the CIA and FBI proved to be true, a large number of these agents began disappearing. As a result of Ames's information, at least ten KGB agents were killed for supplying information to the United States. This is the second largest number of assets to be compromised by one man. Ames was finally arrested just before leaving for a supposedly work-related trip to Moscow. He pleaded guilty and is serving a life sentence for espionage. The information given to the KGB included the names of more than one hundred agents sending Soviet information to the States. Some escaped; some did not.

Chapter 4

Crooked Georgetown

Arrest on the C&O Canal

C orruption in the capital city should not be unexpected. Most cities have a seedy underbelly made up of those longing for easy money. Thousands of dollars in exchange for only the promise of influence or secret bribes from the enemy to deliver privileged information were surely appealing to many. From corporate disloyalty to congressional greed, Georgetown could not escape the scandals. In some cases, the perpetrators were caught, but some may have been innocent all along.

The C&O Canal played a large part in the economic life of Georgetown. During the Civil War, the canal ran along the border between the North and the South, with the front lines crossing back and forth. Battles were fought along the towpath as the Confederacy tried to bring the war further into Union territory. Due to Washington's dependency on the coal transported along the canal from Cumberland mines, it came under the control of the U.S. Army early in the war.

But the fighting took a toll on the canal. The Battles of Gettysburg, Antietam, Balls Bluff, Monocracy and Folcks Mill were fought near enough to the canal that troops from both sides muddied the waters. Knowing its importance to the Union, Confederate troops continually wreaked havoc on the canal resources. Aqueducts from the nearby creeks were destroyed. Three dams, various locks and the steam pump at Potomac Forks were rendered unusable. In the 1860s, mules that walked along the banks towed the boats along the canal. Confederate forces absconded with the mules and burned the boats that were left.

The Union capital may have relied on the coal that came down the canal, but it was just as responsible for damage to the canal as the Confederacy. At one point, Union forces demanded the use of more than one hundred canal boats for the sole purpose of sinking them at the lower end of the Potomac to keep the Confederate ships at bay. In the end, the canal boats were never sunk, but they were kept aside from canal management for some time.

The canal was also used during the war for subversive purposes. It was mostly small tradesmen using the waterways who carried out these actions. At the beginning of the war, Georgetown butcher John Crumbaugh opened a coal-and-wood business along the canal. He successfully ran a smuggling scheme using his canal contacts and the cellar in his N Street NW home until he was caught in 1863.

Due to the canal's importance and location, it was controlled (in theory) by the Union army. However, there was a board and president responsible for the management and well being of the canal. It was, after all, a business. But men in business, especially lucrative businesses in the middle of a war, are always looked at with suspicion. The canal was an important waterway and source of supplies for the Union that the Confederacy would be happy to subjugate. Thus, C&O president Alfred Spates's loyalty to the Union was in question, and when it was found lacking in the slightest, he was imprisoned.

THE UNJUST IMPRISONMENT OF ALFRED SPATES

President Spates was arrested for violating the laws of war. His charge stated:

The specification is, that the accused, on the 6th day of July, 1863, and on divers days before and after that date, did pass from within the lines of the United States Army, and without any proper authority or permission, unlawfully and traitorously, did go within the lines of the Army of the so called Confederate States and into the midst of such Rebel Army, at or near Williamsport and Hagerstown, in Maryland; Martinsburg and Winchester, in Virginia, and other places in Maryland and Virginia, then in rebel occupation; and did hold intercourse with Rebel authorities and procure and receive from General Robert E. Lee, Commanding the Rebel Army, a written pass or permission allowing the accused to pass in and out of the lines of the Rebel army.

To compound this fact, it was added that as president of the canal, he had a relationship with the United States government. An agent of the government seen cavorting with the enemy carried with it a court-martial and punishment of death.

The arresting authorities claimed that Spates had spent the first half of July 1863 crossing into the Confederate-held lands of Hagerstown and Williamsport, Maryland, and through the lines at Winchester and Martinsburg, Virginia. They said that in these locations, he met with Confederate generals Robert E. Lee and Richard Ewell for the purpose of relaying intelligence of the Union army. Nevermind that Williamsport is literally on the C&O Canal, an entity that Spates was in charge of overseeing, and that the towns of Hagerstown and Martinsburg are not far from it. The prosecution found witnesses to Spates's not-so-secret meetings with Confederate officers to support the charge.

In late June 1863, Alfred Spates had word that the road to Frederick from Baltimore was clear of enemy hands. Refugees who had left Hagerstown at the approach of General Lee were returning home. Entering Baltimore were two travelers who assured Spates that the road from Frederick to his destination in Hagerstown was free from Rebel forces, as they had just taken it.

In April of the preceding year, the War Department had issued an order that all officers in the Union army were to assist Spates and not interfere in his role of managing the canal. The same order gave him access to any passes needed to reach the canal. Under presumption of this cooperation, Spates thus decided to try again to reach Hagerstown from Baltimore. He was traveling in his role as president of the C&O Canal without knowledge that there were any Rebel forces in the area. There had been reports of minor damage to some areas of the canal, but the rural area seven miles past Dam 5 had not been surveyed at all. Spates needed firsthand knowledge of the running of his canal.

On July 1, Spates and Miss Sally Roman were in Fredrick. This was a few days before the now famous Battle of Gettysburg, and it was known at the time that the Rebel forces were concentrating in that area of Pennsylvania, leaving the road to Hagerstown accessible. Those residents who had been biding time in Baltimore had returned home, and members of the Union cavalry were in the area, unaware of any Rebel interference.

Spates spent the next few days by the canal surveying the area and any damage left by Confederate troops on the way north. There had been some minor destruction, and Spates was determined to order it repaired

Lockhouse on the C&O Canal. *Library of Congress.*

as soon as possible. When returning from the canal, he heard the sounds of gunshots in the area surrounding Hagerstown. Stopping at the Stake house, it was concluded that there would be no danger in returning to the city. Stake had been there earlier that morning, and it was in the control of the Union troops. Except when Stake took Spates to Hagerstown, they found that the skirmishes outside the city were the result of the Confederate forces retaking it.

The Battle of Gettysburg had been fought, and the retreating Confederate forces under Lee were returning to Hagerstown. The residents quietly stayed, and with no indication of danger, so did Spates. The Rebel forces grew larger as more and more soldiers returned south from Gettysburg into Virginia. As they continued to extend past Hagerstown, Spates found himself within the Confederate lines, but not by choice.

On July 8, Spates came across Charles Marshall, an acquaintance from Baltimore who was now a major in the Confederate army. At this point, Spates acted as president of the C&O Canal and reminded Marshall that the canal was personal property and thus should not be considered necessary or proper to destroy on their way south. And with that, they parted—no government intelligence given.

The following day, the Rebels still controlled the area. With limited provisions now available in Hagerstown, the townsfolk sought to find supplies from local farmers. Spates went with Mr. Roman, an assumed relation to the Miss Roman he accompanied from Baltimore, to an outlying farm for supplies. While there, the famer mentioned that the Confederate army had confiscated part of his property and asked if the two men might intervene on their way back to town. Roman agreed, and he and Spates went to the headquarters of Major Marshall. While Roman was intervening on behalf of the farmer, Spates decided to ask a favor of his old friend. He was now unwittingly in enemy lands. As someone who is known to have special privileges with the Union army, he was afraid of being arrested by the Confederate forces. Spates procured a pass that would allow him some provision of safety while in the area.

With the pass now in hand and Roman's business done, Major Marshall escorted the two back to the cart. Along the way, they passed the tent of General Lee and were introduced. It was not a private meeting, and there were a few townspeople present as well. Few words were passed between Spates and the others before he returned to the city. That was the extent of the events, yet Spates was charged with disloyalty and was forced to argue for his life. In its closing statement, his consul made mention of the fact that many of the state's witnesses had just as much contact with the Rebel army as did Spates, yet none of them were deemed disloyal. Spates believed that he and the canal had enemies in Baltimore.

Though Maryland never seceded from the Union, it was a slave state with many Southern sympathizers. It would not be out of the question that some in Baltimore disliked the canal board, which was under the control of the Union army. There had been previous suspicion that disloyalists used the C&O Canal to aid the Confederates with supplies and information. Brigadier General Benjamin Roberts was in command of troops along the canal but refused to comply with orders to aid Spates and the C&O Canal Company. He had been given information from reliable sources that the company's boats and captains were used to transport contraband along the waterways to the Southern forces. These reliable sources were not identified, and the information came forth only in Roberts's efforts to defend his actions.

Lawrence Brengle and Joseph Bradley, two C&O Canal board members, went to Baltimore to secure the release of Spates, as the evidence against him was coincidental at best. They failed in this endeavor, and Spates was imprisoned for five months. It took a direct order from Secretary of War Edwin Stanton to gain his release. Some historians believe that he had originally been released a month or two after his arrest in September 1863 and then arrested again in January for only a few weeks before being released again on Stanton's orders.

The 1863 arrest for disloyalty was not the first for Spates—or the last. Each time he was arrested following a time that the Confederate forces had been near the canal rather than times he had been near the Confederacy. After each arrest, he was reinstated as president of the C&O Canal.

It seems that unlike many of the families in Georgetown, Spates was quite loyal to the Union. In his case of corruption, in which it was believed that he had given information on the essential workings of the Union use of the canal, the authorities were mistaken. The corruption may not have been his, but it still may have been there. At some point during his 1863 arrest, he had written to the board to ask for additional funds to be sent to him. He stated that $1,000 had already been used and predicted the need for $1,000 more in the near future. In the following months of 1864, Colonel William Fish of the Second Connecticut Calvary was charged with corruption himself. Fish served as the provost marshal of Middle District, where Spates was arrested. He had been, among other illicit acts, arranging for the arrest of citizens and then offering to assist in their release—for a fee, of course.

ABSCAM

Though president Spates of the C&O Canal was proven innocent in his charges of disloyalty to the Union during the Civil War, there was still some corruption to be discovered.

The Federal Bureau of Investigation began its first major operation into thwarting public official corruption in the late 1970s. Kambir Abdul Rahman was a fabulously wealthy Arab sheik seeking asylum in the United States and assistance in retrieving his riches from his home country. He was indifferent to American criminal law and wanted help in any way he could get it—legal or not. The oil-rich sheik met with U.S. senators, representatives, state senators, city councilmen and other government officials in hotel rooms, yachts and a house in the northern part of Georgetown. His company, Abdul Enterprises, had a credit reference from Chase Manhattan Bank and $1 million in its account.

But Rahman was a fake. He was played by FBI agents under the direction of Melvin Weinberg, a former con artist hired to assist in the sting. Weinberg was only participating in the sting to save himself from conviction in his own illegal scheme.

Weinberg had no formal schooling after the eighth grade and spent much of his childhood involved in thievery. He was hired by unions to employ scare tactics on non-union workers. Weinberg's crimes were white collar and involved no physical harm. But this didn't stop him from pretending to be a hit man and collecting cash to kill a woman he had no intention of harming. After being caught dealing in certificates of deposits in offshore banks that never existed, he went from defendant to star witness in taking down U.S. congressmen.

Confident men are likeable, or at least the successful ones are. It's hard not to laugh with the man who talked his way out of an FBI charge and into employment. Weinberg called himself a "creature of habit" when questioned about his two homes (one with his wife and son and the other with his mistress), both of which had the same wallpaper and furniture. When he was arrested by the FBI for wire fraud, he was making $250,000 a year. One year later, he was employed by the FBI and making $150,000. Weinberg was a good conman.

In case the faulty sheik was not suitable, a second man in need was invented. Yasser Habib feared for his life in his home country and suggested that he would heartily thank any congressman who might sponsor a special immigration bill that would grant him asylum in the States. This FBI sting operation, code named the Abdul Scam, or ABSCAM, led to the arrest of six members of Congress.

In videotaped conversations, the wealthy Arabs offered large sums of cash in exchange for the requested favors. Only one congressman, Senator Larry Pressler from South Dakota, turned down the illegal bribe. Pressler immediately reported the incident to the FBI. But of course, they already knew.

Before the sting was carried out, the FBI needed a place to conduct their secret operation. The vacant house of a *Washington Post* reporter who had been transferred to New York City proved ideal. A single man working with the Arlington-based Olympic Construction Corp signed a three-year lease with the provision of making improvements to the house on W Street NW. New recessed lighting, an elaborate alarm system and new wood paneling would all be required. And by recessed lighting, he meant hidden cameras.

Six representatives and one senator were filmed taking cash in exchange for political favors. Using the Georgetown town house, a yacht in Florida and a hotel room in New York City—all outfitted with hidden cameras—all seven congressmen were charged with bribery. Most of the men were Democrats, though Representative Richard Kelly was a Republican. They were former war heroes, lawyers and a regent of the Smithsonian Institute and well liked by their constituents.

Representative Kelly of Florida stuffed $25,000 cash in his pockets and asked the undercover FBI agents if it showed. The eventual ex-wife of Representative John Jenrette of South Carolina found $25,000, half of his bribe, in a shoebox while packing up his things after kicking him out. Pennsylvania representative Raymond Lederer was offered $50,000 in order to introduce a bill allowing the two Arab men to remain in the country. In a moment of honesty, Lederer did declare $5,000 of the bribe as outside income but labeled it as a consulting fee. Frank Thompson, a representative from New Jersey, was the longest serving member of Congress indicted in ABSCAM, having served thirteen terms. He received $50,000 for the anticipated private immigration bill. Thompson brought into the scheme Representative John Murphy of New York.

The representatives were convicted of bribery and conspiracy and resigned from their positions in Congress. Murphy was acquitted. Though most believed that he knew there was money in the briefcase presented to him, he made no promises as to what he would do to earn it. Although Thompson was not present when Murphy accepted their bribes, he did follow through on actions in the interest of the Arab sheiks. He said he would bring in another party, and he did. Murphy was charged with accepting an unlawful gratuity, a lesser charge. Thompson was sentenced to the maximum of fifteen years in prison, though he served only two. He had been defeated in his 1980 reelection campaign. Murphy was sentenced to three years in prison and also lost his reelection.

Lederer and Myers were also sentenced to three years. Lederer was the only congressman to be reelected after the ABSCAM scandal, winning with 54.5 percent of the vote. Apparently, Pennsylvania's third congressional district really disliked his opponents. But with the threat of expulsion by the House Ethics Committee, Lederer resigned due to personal legal problems. Myers did not resign but was officially expelled from Congress later that year by a House Resolution with a vote of 376–30. This was the first time since 1861 that a House member was expelled.

Jenrette lost his reelection and resigned shortly before the end of his term. He was sentenced to two years in prison and served just over one. To add to his scandalous legacy, he and his wife, Rita, were rumored to have had a salacious tryst on the steps of the Capitol Building behind one of the pillars—though Rita now says that never happened.

Kelly spent thirteen months in prison and lost his reelection. While most of the congressmen maintained their innocence and called the sting operation entrapment, Kelly had a unique defense. Yes, he accepted the money, but not because he was corrupt. Rather, he was trying to weed out corruption in his own undercover mission. He spent some of the bribe in order to protect his cover and convince the others that they had him under their control. In reality, he had always planned on turning them over to the FBI.

One representative was not filmed accepting the bribe but nearly did. John Murtha of Pennsylvania did meet with the supposed sheik. His claim was that he was pursuing potential investments in his district. In all likelihood, he knew there would be cash involved. He had been told prior by Representative Thompson that the sheiks would be providing $50,000 in walking-around money. But he never accepted the money and was never indicted.

The only member of the Senate to be indicted was Senator Harrison "Pete" Williams of New Jersey. Williams never accepted a cash bribe but did agree to an 18 percent share in a titanium mine. In exchange for his portion of the venture, he would use his position to influence government contracts.

ABSCAM support letter. *Courtesy of Federal Bureau of Investigation.*

He was found guilty and served two out of his sentenced three years in prison. The Senate formally censured him, but he resigned his seat before they could vote to expel him.

Though those indicted were convicted and their sentences upheld at appeals, some thought the FBI tactics came close to entrapment. The result was more organized rules for undercover operations as outlined by the Department of Justice. Public support was split between those who supported the FBI's actions and those who thought the actions were corrupt themselves. The records at the FBI do a good job of preserving those that show a positive public opinion on its actions.

Had General Lee had a hidden video camera in his tent while in Hagerstown, Maryland, perhaps we would know exactly what information Alfred Spates passed on to the Confederacy that day. Luckily for the president of the C&O Canal, the video camera had not been invented yet, though it seems that it would have proven him innocent anyways. But for the six members of Congress, the footage taken in Georgetown did little to prove their innocence.

Chapter 5

Murder on the Canal

The Stories of John Bruebaker and Mary Meyer

The C&O Canal has more than a century of history to share, and it can't all be good. For the time it served as an industrial hub, the characters that lived and worked on the canal were of a coarser nature. As the industry moved away and the elite moved back in, the canal became what it is today—a peaceful path through ivy-covered brick buildings…peaceful unless someone wants you dead.

A Boatman's Brawl

Canal workers on the C&O Canal in the nineteenth century had a reputation of being rough-and-tumble men, fast on assumptions and quick to the fist. The canal stretched nearly 190 miles along the Potomac River between Cumberland, Maryland, and Georgetown. Canal boatmen worked long hours, garnered little pay and were unrefined, especially when compared to the high-class lot of Georgetown. Brawls were common, and no matters were more serious than those regarding their women. In Georgetown in March 1886, boatmen George Seaman and John Bruebaker were no exception to this description.

The story unfolds like a film in which you aren't sure who the good guy is—if there is one at all. John Bruebaker and George Seaman were drunks.

They were friends but fought with each other often. In what was likely a common occurrence, George Seaman was at home sleeping off the effects of his latest night out. Seaman lived at 3315 Water Street (present-day K Street NW). It wasn't a residence all his own, and upstairs on the third floor lived a Mrs. Epps. That evening, Mrs. Bruebaker had escorted home her friend Mrs. Epps only to find that she had fallen ill upon their arrival. Obliged to call for assistance, Mrs. Bruebaker was able to rouse Seaman and entreat his assistance.

And as would be predicted, John Bruebaker staggered in drunk the moment George Seaman was in the room with Mrs. Bruebaker and Mrs. Epps. Bruebaker had already told his wife before not to be caught in this particular house again. Yet here she was. He was a man primed for a fight and drunk out of his wits. Bruebaker reeled back and struck his wife squarely in the face. Despite her pleas and the presence of witnesses of this domestic abuse, Bruebaker wound up for another. At that very instant, Seaman lunged forward before the blow could be struck. This was his moment of chivalry.

It seems that Mrs. Bruebaker was accustomed to these abuses. As each man sized up the other for the inevitable brawl, she intervened to drag her husband away. She claimed that she was able to handle any blow her husband dealt her. Seaman headed out of the room, but Bruebaker couldn't leave well enough alone. He reportedly belted out to his wife, "Seaman is . the bully of Georgetown, but he can't whip me!" Seaman rushed back to the room in a rage, and the two men fought it out.

With his decidedly advantageous sobriety, Seaman beat Bruebaker about the face while the wife clung to his arms pleading for the pummeling to end. Despite his abuse, she continued to claim that she could take it and insisted that Seaman leave her husband alone. She was not as passive as the refined ladies of Georgetown. Mrs. Bruebaker rushed Seaman and held back his arms, giving her husband the chance to become the aggressor. But this also gave Seaman the chance to kick Bruebaker squarely in the stomach and send him flying across the room where he fell, unable to get up.

The fight was over, but the ordeal was not. The still drunk and now badly hurt Bruebaker had to be carried out of the house and onto a boat not far behind. It was nothing new, until he slipped into unconsciousness. Though the physician was immediately called, it was too late. John Bruebaker died a few hours later at six o'clock in the morning from a rupture in his abdomen.

The appropriate authorities were called and Seaman arrested for the murder of John Bruebaker. The autopsy report suggested the he had knocked Bruebaker down and stomped on him, contrary to the witness reports of

Bridge and boat along the C&O Canal. *Library of Congress.*

Bruebaker's wife and Mrs. Epps. Regardless of the exact circumstances, it was determined that his injuries were the result of the violence George · Seaman had inflicted on him during the fight that evening.

It was less than a month later, on April 7, 1886, that the verdict on George Seaman was read. Despite the witness testimonies, he was not convicted of manslaughter. Newspaper reports of the incident stated that this was the third man Seaman had killed. The circumstances of these previous events are unknown, but at any rate, the power and patience of this man was obviously not to be tested.

This undoubtedly was not the first fight that John Bruebaker had been in, but it was also not the first in which he had suffered. In September 1876, Bruebaker had it out with an Alphonso Arrington in Cumberland, Maryland, at the other end of the C&O Canal. Arrington was known for two things: a proclivity for drunken fighting and a passion for dogfights. He and Bruebaker were discussing the virtues of their belligerent beasts when it became apparent that Bruebaker thought his of better quality. A fight ensued between Arrington and Bruebaker with the former gnawing off the right ear of the latter. Arrington was later arrested in his escape to Washington, but for unknown reasons, Bruebaker decided not to prosecute.

Just as it wasn't Bruebaker's first, it wasn't Seaman's last. A few years later, a George Seaman was in the police court yet again. The only indication that it might be the same man is a statement by a newspaper reporter that Seaman had "figured in the Police Court several times recently." In April 1890, he filed suit against Mr. W.S. Branson for a threat against him and was being countersued by the same under a similar accusation. An exasperated judge ordered both to pay a $200 bond and be done with the matter.

Earlier in January of that same year, Seaman was seen in court under the charge of profanity for having called a Mr. Horn "some hard names" at Horn's place of work. From the newspaper reports, it seems that Mr. Seaman was not a pleasure to have in the courtroom. This particular judge had to stop Seaman, as he continued too long and in too much detail for the court's taste and was charged a five-dollar fine or jail. He chose to pay.

These rough-and-tumble men of the C&O Canal may not have made Georgetown their place of permanent residence, but neither did the wealthy socialites in town only for the social season. Surely John Bruebaker and George Seaman were not the only troublemakers found in the Georgetown courts. But these canal boatmen did leave their mark—the soot from the coal they transported and the blood from the fights they often had—on the white satin papers of Georgetown's history.

The Mysterious Murder of Mary Meyer

The canal was not just witness to the death of boatmen killed in fights. In 1964, the Georgetown Canal was the scene of a grisly murder. In what may be the most salacious murder mystery in this historic neighborhood, there has been no answer to the question of who killed Mary Meyer.

Mary Meyer was the ex-wife of CIA official Cord Meyer; the daughter of the wealthy and political Pinochet family; sister-in-law to Ben Bradlee, editor of the *Washington Post*; and supposed mistress to her neighbor, John F. Kennedy. She was a connected woman in the social and political scene, which led to both shock and conspiracies surrounding her murder.

For the personal safety of the author, no personal opinions will be formed. If the conspiracy theories are true and it was a CIA operation, it's better to be safe than sorry! There are two main opinions on what happened that day on the C&O Canal. Some believe that Mary was murdered by Ray Crump Jr., who was arrested but later acquitted, while others believe that she had discovered too much about the assassination of JFK.

Mary Meyer's studio above the garage. *Author's collection.*

Mary was a well-known artist in the Georgetown community and used a studio loft over the Bradlees' garage at their N Street NW home. On the afternoon of October 12, 1964, Mary went for her customary stroll along the canal for fresh air and inspiration. That afternoon, a car mechanic had been dispatched to tow a stalled Nash Rambler sedan near the canal. As he reached the area, he heard the sounds of a woman shouting. Before he could get closer to the edge of the road that overlooked the canal, there were two gunshots in quick succession. Looking over the wall, he saw a woman crumpled on the canal towpath and a man standing over her. The man was black and wearing a cap, dark trousers and a beige-colored jacket, and in his hand he had what appeared to be a weapon. He was not startled or panicked but rather coolly surveyed the moment and calmly walked away.

Meanwhile, a short distance down the canal, Ray Crump Jr. had fallen in—at least that was his story. He claimed to have been fishing and drinking when he fell asleep and slipped into the canal, losing his equipment. When he was met by the police walking down the tracks on the far side of the canal, he had on no cap or jacket, but he was a black male with dark trousers. The police took him into custody—something about his story did not seem right. No fishing equipment was ever found, but the police did find a beige jacket in the Potomac River that fit him perfectly and a cap along the banks of the canal. How a jacket that was supposedly tossed in the canal made it to that side of the Potomac River was never clarified, but no one in the police department seemed too concerned about that discrepancy. A neighbor of Crump's had seen him that morning leaving his house in a beige jacket, a baseball cap and with no fishing pole.

Crump had lied to the police about his reasons for being on the canal, and that did not help his case. The rule is innocent until proven guilty, and there was a lack of evidence to prove him guilty. He obviously was not fishing in the canal, at least with his own equipment, but that does not mean he murdered Mary Meyer. In addition, the mechanic had given a description of a much larger man that did not match Crump's small frame.

But there are still those who believe that it was Crump. The courts could neither prove nor disprove that he did. He had no alibi, and there were suspicious circumstances regarding his proximity to the murder scene. But let's say the diminutive fisherman had a few too many beers and slipped into the canal, losing his cap, jacket and the pole he borrowed from a friend—then who killed Mary Meyer?

Mary was a mistress of JFK. Mary and Cord Meyer were well established in the social scene of Georgetown and were friends with the Kennedys.

Mary's sister and brother-in-law, the Bradlees, lived a few doors down from the Kennedys' pre-presidential home. JFK had a penchant for beautiful women, and Mary was one of them. Furtive glances at social functions, visits to the White House after his election and rumors of the affair after their deaths led to the possibility that there was indeed a real relationship.

After Mary and her CIA agent husband divorced, she went from 1950s housewife to 1960s acid trip. Timothy Leary, of LSD and "turn on, tune in, drop out" fame, was a friend and supplier. He claims that the love affair between Mary and JFK included acid trips that were helping to turn the president into a "peace and love" kind of politician. Essentially, they were turning him into the kind of pacifist that the CIA did not want to interfere with their foreign policy monopoly.

Then, on a trip to Dallas in November 1963, President John F. Kennedy was shot. Assuming that it was not Lee Harvey Oswald in the book depository and that the CIA did consider JFK's increasing concern with the military strength as a threat (and as stated before, this is just a hypothetical statement), it could have been a CIA operation.

If the inquisitive and well-connected lover of JFK became too enthralled in the mystery of his assassination, it could end badly. She was reported to have kept a notebook of newspaper clippings relating to the event. What did she learn?

Mary was shot twice—once cleanly in the head and once in the back. She was shot with such professional precision that it was an instantaneous death. The medical examiner believed the shooter meant to kill her. It took hours for the police to identify the woman shot on the canal, but Mary's friends (you know, the ones who worked at the CIA) knew it was her before the police did. A witness came forward stating that he had seen Crump walking along the towpath in the direction of Mary Meyer. William Mitchell was jogging on the canal when he passed Mary with Crump walking toward her before he heard the gunshots. As an employee at the Pentagon, Mitchell was a credible witness. But the timeline and distances he gave don't add up. The stalled car that the other witness went to fix had mysteriously disappeared after he finished giving his report to the police. Mary's diary went missing after her death. It was reportedly either burned by her sister or turned over to the CIA by Ben Bradlee, though one investigator claimed to have found it.

Leo Damore said he located a copy of the diary. He also claimed that he had a confession from a CIA operative who admitted to the deed—the same William Mitchell who testified at Crump's trial. Damore committed suicide

Towpath along the C&O Canal, Georgetown. *Author's collection.*

in the 1990s while researching Mary Meyer's case for a new book before any information about Mitchell was turned over to authorities. Mitchell has since disappeared. Could the CIA have killed Damore, too? It was not a staged suicide; there were witnesses. This would mean that the CIA was able perform psychological maneuvering to get Damore to commit suicide because he knew too much about the murder of Mary Meyer, who knew too much about JFK's assassination. At the time of this writing, the most recent research regarding this conspiracy is documented in Peter Janney's *Mary's Mosaic.* Janney is still alive.

Chapter 6

Scalded

The Tragic Death of the Spong Children

Those who traversed the C&O Canal for a living assumed the stereotype of being brawny fighting men. However, there were also women and children who traveled up and down the waterways with their husbands. These rough-and-tumble women had a similar reputation of being unrefined but worked hard to keep the boats in working order with a homey feel.

One of the families working on the canal was that of Captain Samuel Spong of Sharpsburg, Maryland. Captain Spong and his wife, Nina, had four children who stayed with them on the canal. Thomas, the eldest child, tended the work with his father, but the three younger children, aged six to thirteen, were mostly along for the ride. Like many of the canal boatmen, the Spongs' barge number 74 was bringing in coal. Delivering for the Consolidation Coal Company, they docked at the Capital Traction Plant in Georgetown on the morning of September 11, 1916.

The Capitol Traction Company was a transit company that operated the streetcars running through Washington, D.C., and Georgetown. With car barns and trolley tracks throughout the city, the company had been a presence in Georgetown since the late 1800s. Originally using horse-drawn carriages, the company eventually evolved with modern times and developed an electric streetcar. These were noticeably cleaner than the horses but required power to move along the tracks. To this end, a power plant was built along the waterfront in Georgetown. The location allowed easy access

View of the Capital Traction Plant from the Potomac River. *Library of Congress.*

to the coal coming in and a presumably safe place to release the by-products of the power process. The Capital Traction Plant was just over four years old in 1916, still utilizing the new pipes and fittings installed at its opening.

There were twelve boilers to operate the generators that produced and sent out the electrical current through the city to run these earliest forms of public transportation. Each morning, the night engineers and firemen on duty would open a valve that allowed the built-up steam pressure to escape from the boilers. The excess steam and hot water barrelled through the pipes of the plant and were released into the Potomac River. Every morning for four years at 4:30 a.m. and 6:00 a.m., the pipes were blown out, and the plant could begin powering the streetcars.

Barge 74, with the Spong family aboard, was tugged out of the C&O Canal through the Rock Creek lock into the Potomac River and to the loading dock. The barge was the Spongs' means of living, but it was also their home. It had a small cabin in which the family slept. Despite the preparations for the day, the children remained asleep in the wee hours of the morning. The boat was anchored to the loading dock just before 6:00 a.m. along the concrete slab just opposite the power plant, whose pipes pointed down to the river.

The C&O Canal. *Library of Congress.*

Captain Spong, his wife and their eldest son were beginning their day by cooking breakfast on the boat and preparing to unload the coal. This was a routine practiced for years at a location no newer to him than his own boat. That morning, Captain Spong "knew of no danger in the world," as he would later recall in testimony.

That is, until he heard the screams.

His three youngest children on the boat had been sleeping in the cabin with the screens and wooden shutters closed over the windows. At 6:00 a.m., as had been done every other day as part of the duty at the plant, the valves for the exhaust pipe were opened. Thomas Rollins was in charge of Boiler No. 3 that night. The boiler had three valves, and though it was routine to turn them one at a time, he turned the second while the first one was still on. The process usually took six minutes to blow out all the steam. Today, it was less than a minute.

The hot air from the boiler released through the shaking pipes as it made its way down and out of the plant. The pipe was meant to come out of the wall and bend down through an elbow joint to point directly at the river. But this morning, it did not.

Captain Spong and Thomas Rollins were simply doing what they had always done. But on September 11, 1916, the pressure of the steam burst through the elbow joint and did not shoot down to the river. It shot straight out and through the shutters and screens of the cabin window.

The three Spong children awoke to the scalding steam and hot water from the boilers but were unable to get out of the cabin. With motherly instincts, Nina Spong sprung into action, but she was too soon after the initial blast and too slow to escape being burned herself. Captain Spong attempted to run into the cabin, burning himself on the back in the process, but was pushed aside by his eldest son. Thomas rushed in to save his brothers and sister. He began handing his father the burned bodies of his siblings with their torn and disintegrating clothes. At one point, he had to stop from going back into the cabin, not being able to breath himself due to suffocation from the heavy steam. The father recalled one moment when one of his young sons ran to the cabin window, unable to escape. He saw the boy screaming in agony through the glass before his brother could reach him. It took them ten minutes to get everyone out of the cabin and away from the hissing steam.

When the police arrived, every member of the Spong family had been burned in some way and had inhaled the thick, scalding steam. The three youngest children did not survive the night at Georgetown Hospital. Sarah Spong, only six years old, died within four hours. John, age thirteen, died within six hours, and Samuel, age eleven, later that afternoon. Nina Spong spent months in the hospital, missing the funeral of her three children, but she did survive.

During the inquest and trial, the Capital Traction Company, as expected of a large corporation, had lawyers and legal teams to assist in proving their innocence. Despite this, the jury decided that this tragedy was an accident caused by the company's negligence. One of the firemen that night, William Wiggington, admitted that the safety valve of his boiler had turned off around 6:00 a.m. that day, despite his blowing off the boiler steam earlier that morning. Rollins had already been formally arrested on the day of the event, as he was the one who had turned on the steam. Initial reports have him denying any responsibility at first and claiming that it must have been someone else.

In the end, there were three men there that morning—engineers and firemen in charge of blowing off the steam. William Wiggington, Thomas Rollins and Virgil Walker did their jobs as they always did. The steam on this particular morning was less than normal and thus it look less time to blow off than it usually did. For the Spong children, however, there was little difference between one minute and six. Perhaps six minutes of straight steam and hissing hot water would have resulted in quicker deaths and less suffering. Rollins may have had two valves open at once. The safety valves of any of the three boilers may have been off. But it was not these individuals who were determined at fault.

During the trial, John Hanna, a former chief engineer and now vice-president for the company, admitted that the elbow joint was not the type typically used for main boiler lines. In addition, when asked if he had taken into account the pressure involved in releasing vast amounts of steam, he admitted that he hadn't. He attempted to justify this by stating that those types of elbow joints were made to withstand such pressure. When shown the pipe in court, Mr. Hanna determined that there was some wear in the elbow, as the threads had been rounded off. The police had decided on the day of the tragedy that the fitting could not have been too worn since the plant was relatively new. But the wear and tear of a piece is irrelevant if the piece was not meant for that purpose in the first place.

As reported in Washington County's *Daily Mail*, the verdict was issued two days later on September 13. How is that for speedy justice? The verdict stated:

> *The coroner's jury investigating the cause of the Spong children's death rendered a verdict of the tragedy due to "Accident." It supplemented its verdict with a statement that the accident was due to the Capitol Traction Company's failure to provide safe connection of exhaust pipe for steam and hot water at the powerhouse.*

John, Samuel and Sarah Spong are buried together in Mountain View Cemetery in Sharpsburg, Maryland. A funeral attended by many saw the three smallest coffins lowered into the ground. Their headstone still stands today, even if the tragedy of what happened to them has been forgotten.

It may have nothing to do with this tragic family, but there is a rock along the Potomac River that perhaps is a reminder of the family's

Headstone of the Spong children. *Author's collection.*

time on the canal. At Lock 16 at Great Falls, miles upriver from Georgetown, is a sandstone block with letters carved into it. In what looks to be a child's handwriting are the letters W-S-P-O-N-G. It's hard to say for sure, but it could be the markings of the young Samuel Spong, who went by his middle name of Willard.

Chapter 7

Scandalous Love

The Bodisco Marriage

As the hamlet of Georgetown grew alongside the capital, it became a place of residence for foreign dignitaries hoping to include themselves in the upper echelons of society. Marriage between prominent families to secure wealth, reputation, land and good name was all too common in Georgetown. Soon, members of the diplomatic corps were marrying into these families to secure a position in American society.

But sometimes, it was not just a marriage of convenience. In fact, it was very inconvenient that Baron Bodisco fell in love with Harriet Williams. It was not that she was already married or promised to another—nor was her family too poor for it to be a positive match for the Russian minister. Harriet's father was only a government clerk and thus they were not the most socially influential or richest of families, but they were descended from one of the founders of Georgetown—Ninian Beall. The Williamses were well off enough to educate Harriet at Miss English's Seminary for Young Ladies. This was the same school that was run by the ardent secessionist, but Harriet attended the school long before the Civil War. At this time, Miss English was only educating Georgetown ladies in the hospitable ways for which Southern ladies were and still are known. Even Andrew Jackson sent his daughter here while he served as a Tennessee senator. In fact, Harriet Williams was still a student at the school when Baron Bodisco proposed. That is what made it inconvenient. Young Harriet was sixteen years old; Baron Bodisco was nearly in his sixties.

Baron Alexander de Bodisco served as Russian ambassador for seventeen years. His official title was Envoy Extraordinary and Minister Plenipotentiary, and he had the reputation of living up to such a lofty designation. From his home in Georgetown, he would ride in a white carriage drawn by four black horses to the Russian Embassy. He was known to have a pretentious air about him, and this was compounded by the fact that he either dyed his hair or wore a wig. The baron was said to have a squat ugliness, but he was a brilliant courtier, and his looks were countered by his charm.

In his role as representative of Russia and the court of Czar Nicolas, Baron Bodisco threw lavish parties and made his way around the card tables with other members of the diplomatic corps. One of these parties was a more familial affair in which he threw a Christmas celebration for his two nephews studying at Georgetown College. The two young boys, Boris and Waldemar Bodisco, studied medicine with Dr. Joshua Riley in town. It was a grand affair with toys, candies and lavish decorations around the Bodisco mansion. Bonfires lit the way along the streets to the house to ward against the darkness and the chill. There was even a Santa Claus to hand out gifts to the children. The party was thrown for all the youth of Georgetown, but Harriet Williams was mistakenly not invited. This unfortunate error was corrected by the baron himself with a note of apology and invitation. At the party, he sought her out to offer a personal apology.

In the days following the party, Baron Bodisco could be seen waiting for Harriet along the road leading to her school at Miss English's. Much to the delight of her classmates, the gentleman would take her books and escort her to class. These daily dalliances eventually led to a proposal of marriage. Soon afterward, the gossip and scandal of it all began. Harriet Williams was a known beauty in Georgetown. A youthful and blossoming girl of sixteen was now being courted by a stout, whiskered and much older Russian diplomat. There were those who disapproved of the marriage due to the Baron's age, namely Harriet's family, but Harriet and her friends relished the fairy tale.

It was only a few months earlier that Harriet Williams had been duly elected by her classmates as May Queen for the celebrations at Miss English's seminary. But when the time came for the announcement, it was the name of another student that was called by the teacher. Harriet's friend, Jessie Benton, daughter of a Missouri senator, denounced the unjustness of it all. She concluded that the change was due to the societal status of Harriet's family and her father's clerical job. From someone not good enough to be a May Queen for a day in a school pageant, Harriet Williams was soon to become a real-life baroness.

Baron Bodisco was aware of the unlikelihood that the youthful Harriet was passionately in love with him. He admitted that he was not the most attractive suitor but stated that none would love her as much as he. And surely, the generosity he showed to her family and friends did not hurt. The Williams family eventually relented to the baron's proposal. He was happy to assist in educating the many children and providing for their future after their father passed away.

It would be wrong to suggest that the young lady chose her husband out of pettiness and desire to be spoiled. It was surely a pleasant revenge to the other schoolgirls who looked down upon her family. And what young girl doesn't dream of a prince sweeping her off in a white carriage? If any of this had a role in her initial decision, Harriet Williams redeemed herself as a loving and faithful wife. The Baron and Baroness Bodisco had seven children together and were happily married for fourteen years until his sudden death. But the happy ending of this fairy tale was not yet known to the gossips at the time, who called the couple "Beauty and the Beast."

If the couple's May–December romance was not enough to talk about, the wedding would prove to be the event of the season. Baron Bodisco took it upon himself to make it an affair to remember and one well deserving of his beautiful bride-to-be. The bridesmaids were friends of Harriet's and thus were all in their mid-teens as well. He ordered the dresses for each of the girls and instructed them on how to carry themselves during the wedding. To compliment the young bridesmaids, the groomsmen were distinguished men of a more advanced age like the baron. Not all of Harriet's friends could make the event. One of them had to forgo her bridesmaid station after the accidental drowning of her brother, Lafayette Miller. Remaining were seven youthful girls in white satin and lace, her sister among them. Each girl received as a gift a ring with her favorite stone.

The older groomsmen included noted government officials. The British minister, Henry Fox, attended as a groomsman despite his reputation for sleeping through the day in order to stay out at night. The ministers from the Netherlands, Austria and Texas also stood with Baron Bodisco. At this point, Texas was an independent republic and thus had its own ambassadors in the district. Senator James Buchanan, who would later become president, had the honor of being a groomsman, as did the sons of the secretary of the navy and secretary of state.

During an unusually sunny day in the midst of April showers, the ceremony was held in the Williams's home, crowded with military men in full uniform, ambassadors, legates and even the president and his

Bodisco House at 3322 O Street NW. *Library of Congress.*

cabinet. The wedding party was arranged in a horseshoe fashion, with the bridesmaids and groomsmen coupled. Baron Bodisco stood at the center and wore his blue court attire with silver lace. Senator Henry Clay presented Harriet to be married. Her wedding dress, designed in the Russian fashion, was a creamy white with a rare lace and red velvet coronet embedded with diamonds. The bride and bridesmaids all wore gifts of pearls. Harriet was adorned with gemstones and jewels of Bodisco heritage sent over from Russia for the occasion.

Following the ceremony were dinners for the bridal party and families. The next few days were filled with amusements for the young bride and her friends. With every drawer opened, a new treasure was found as they explored the house. Gold coins, jewels and candies from France filled an old secretary desk in the bedroom.

A dinner hosted by President Van Buren was eventually arranged in the newlyweds' honor at the White House. Madame Bodisco, as she was now called, wore black silk trimmed with pearls. Later dinners saw her arrive in diamonds with small, freshly cut rosebuds embroidered onto her clothes. Harriet led the real fairy-tale life, complete with jewels befitting a princess.

Following were years of happy marriage. The Bodisco House, located on O Street NW, was a gift to the bride from her husband. The home became the site of many social events during their marriage. After witnessing the happiness of both husband and wife and the successful marriage, gossip about the romance soon faded. The expenses of the baron, the beauty of his wife and the parties they hosted together remained the talk of the town.

Before Baron Bodisco died, he made it clear that he wished Harriet to continue her life as a beautiful woman and to find someone to make her as happy as she had made him. Alexander de Bodisco died at the couple's house on O Street NW in 1854. He is buried in Oak Hill Cemetery in Georgetown. Shortly after the baron's death, Harriet Williams Bodisco married a British officer, Captain Douglas Scott, and lived a second "happily ever after."

Chapter 8

Forbidden Love

The Nuns of Georgetown

O ne might not expect to find a chapter about nuns in a book describing the scandalous side of Georgetown. The women of the Monastery of Visitation in Georgetown are no doubt to be commended for their piety and service to the community. But in the 1800s, the arrival and, in one case, departure of a select few nuns got the rumor mill grinding, and the whispers of gossip would be heard throughout the streets of Georgetown.

VIRGINIA SCOTT: THE GENERAL'S PIOUS DAUGHTER

Virginia Scott was the second (and favorite) daughter of General Winfield Scott. General Scott was a man of considerable military talent who had fought in the Mexican War and commanded Union troops during the Civil War. He was revered by some and despised by others. Confederate spy Thomas Conrad, who we discussed in Chapter 3, had planned to assassinate him, and William O. Williams was hanged as a suspected spy partly because the Union was still angry with him for leaving as General Scott's personal secretary. It is not just that a famous general's daughter joined the sisters at this particular Georgetown convent that

Georgetown Visitation Monastery. *Library of Congress.*

stirred this story, though that is certainly part of the reason why it was so well recorded.

Virginia was beautiful and intelligent, with a special talent for foreign languages. She excelled in her studies and was the envy of her peers. Though endowed with intelligence, beauty and a famous father, Virginia did not boast or use these attributes with ulterior motives. She was a compassionate young woman without the sin of pride. Virginia would be the ideal nun.

After moving to Paris with her mother and sister, Virginia discovered the Catholic faith. Her family was staying within the Convent of the Sacred Heart, and through observance of the nuns, Virginia realized her path to Catholicism. She converted in Rome in 1843, much to the dismay of her Protestant father.

But no amount of virtue or faith can keep a teenage girl from falling in love. And to Virginia's credit, it's hard not to fall in love in Paris. She met a man of high standing who shared with her a devotion to the Catholic faith. They were to be married and live a life full of social graces, Catholic masses and beautiful children. However, to follow societal expectations of marriage and children was against her soul's desire. Virginia wanted nothing more than to fully commit herself to the education of her spiritual knowledge. Her beau felt the same. Rather than a matrimonial ceremony and a life of wedded bliss, the two youths expressed their love for each other through their love for God.

Virginia decided to join the convent at the Georgetown Visitation and take the veil. This meant renouncing worldly possessions and separating from her betrothed and from her beloved father. The nuns were confined to the convent, and rarely were visitors let in.

To have lost his daughter to a different faith was one thing, but now the poor General Scott was to lose his daughter to the convent. No amount of persuasion or entreaties from her parents convinced her of a different path. Virginia Scott entered the convent to become Sister Mary Emmanuel. The convent remarked at her piety. She was often found kneeling in prayer. A youthful twenty-two years of age, Virginia was among the most obedient, cheerful and grateful postulants. But this was not to last long.

In the monastic tradition, a woman newly entered into the convent must wait one year before taking her solemn vows. Virginia Scott was a frail woman and became more so throughout her tenure at Georgetown Visitation. Before a year was up, at month ten, it was decided that her vows should not be put off. Owing to her selflessness and committed spirit, she was allowed to take her vows two months early.

Though the convent grounds are generally closed to the public, when a nun is ill, her family is allowed to attend to her. This was the case when General Winfield Scott paid a visit to his failing but still favorite daughter. It was the last time he would see her. On the very day of her profession, Virginia Scott glowed with a heavenly peace given to her by the final measure of devotion to God and the Catholic faith. She slipped in and out of consciousness, holding tight to her crucifix, only to open her eyes when it was held to her lips. Her last words spoken as she kissed the crucifix were, "Jesus, the God of my heart." She slipped away the very day she fulfilled her deepest wish to become a nun.

To the delight of Georgetown diary keepers, Virginia was the fodder for much talk. Born the daughter of a well-known military and Protestant family, she fell in love with a Parisian boy, with the Catholic faith and with service to God. None of these appealing to her family or her famous father, she was not to be strewn from her presumed fate. In the case of Virginia Scott, she did not so much run away from love—she ran to the nunnery in spite of it.

BERTHA GEROLT:
THE CHILDREN MUSTN'T BE CATHOLIC!

Bertha Gerolt joined the nunnery with less purity of spirit than Virginia Scott. Angered by her family and embarrassed by her fiancé, she felt the convent was her only option.

Baron von Gerolt was the Prussian Ambassador to the United States. It was common for statesmen and their families to settle in the wealthier neighborhoods of Georgetown. When Baron and Madame von Gerolt first arrived in the States, their English being poor, they were subject to the assistance of others for communication and learning. Among the diplomacy of the political world and stiff collars, there is a sense of humor to be found. Having been taught it as a proper introduction, Baron von Gerolt greeted new acquaintances with a rousing, "I'm damned glad to see you."

Gerolt's two daughters, Bertha and Dorothea, were belles of the ball with grace, poise, beauty and proper English. It would not be long before they were both married off within the ranks of the diplomatic world. Dorothea married and followed her political husband to be stationed in Greece. Bertha's story, however, is composed entirely of rumors. Few of them proved to be true, with the exception that she was to fall in love but never marry.

A handsome young man made his intentions known to the lovely Bertha, then twenty-three years old. He was supposedly the heir to a large estate in northern Prussia, a relation of the Bismarck and a descendant of the wealthy Brandenburg family. With each telling of the story, he became more dashing, wealthier and of better familial stock. He was also Protestant. His inheritance of the large ancestral homestead in Prussia was subject to the continuation of his Protestant faith and that of his heirs.

The Gerolts were Catholic—not so staunchly that they could not accept a man of a different faith, but enough that they would need the church's permission to do so. Baron von Gerolt, like any doting father of a beautiful girl, wrote to the Catholic Church for permission for his daughter to marry a Protestant. It was not so much the faith of Bertha's beloved that dissuaded the church from issuing the agreement but rather the stipulation that the children were to be raised Protestant.

From the local church authorities to the pope in Rome, no official church consent was granted. By the time it was decided, however, it didn't much matter. With all the waiting for permission and the bickering between the two families, the engagement was dissolved. The young Prussian fiancé gave up and went back to his Lutheran homestead. The

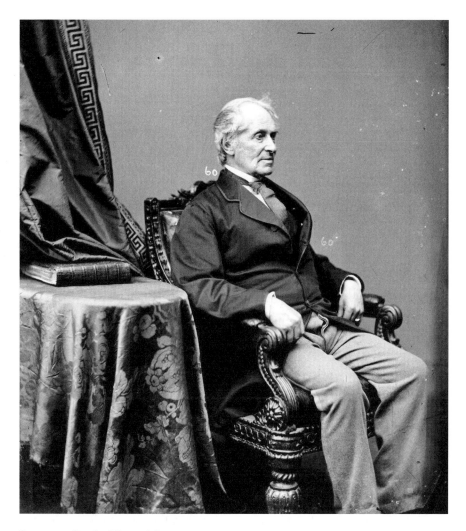

Baron von Gerolt. *Library of Congress.*

devastated Bertha gave up, too. In late 1871, she entered the Convent of Georgetown Visitation, where she remained as Sister Angela until her death some nineteen years later.

But who was this mysterious, larger-than-life Prussian fellow who stole young Bertha Gerolt's heart? Each story gives a different name, most of them not very plausible. We are first told that it was Baron von Gerolt's secretary of legation, Baron Grabow (Grabeur), who in all likelihood was wealthy, handsome and most definitely Prussian. However, he was also married to an American woman named Nina Wood. While one cannot be certain, it is highly unlikely that the Catholic father would request the pope to grant an out-of-faith marriage to an already married man. Divorced *and* Protestant—oh my!

An alternate theory suggests that the young man was well-known to the general public of the time as he was engaged in a duel with "one of our ministers, Lawrence, of Central America." The author of this statement had his facts blatantly confused. General Albert Gallatin Lawrence, minister to Costa Rica, discovered letters between his wife and the Honorable Amedee Van den Nest of Belgium. These letters acted as evidence of an affair, and Lawrence challenged Van den Nest to a duel. He traveled to Belgium, where a bloodless duel satisfied the men's requisite for honorable actions. Lawrence returned to the States and divorced his wife, who married Van den Nest and lived happily ever after. All of this happened after Bertha Gerolt became a nun.

There is another option that may prove to have been Bertha's lost lover. It is one Chevalier Abraham Pieter Cornelis van Karnebeek of the Netherlands. So this one wasn't Prussian, but he was honorable. Karnebeek was the son of a Dutch politician and governor-general of the Dutch East Indies, and he had an illustrious career in the Dutch government as minister of foreign affairs and later minister of state. His family's wealth and political status meant that they might have traveled in similar circles as the Prussian legation. Though it seems no Karnebeek had much to do with America—much less Georgetown—the two young lovebirds could have fallen for each other in Europe. Karnebeek would have been thirty-four years old at the time and Bertha twenty-three—by no means an unusual age difference in that day. Karnebeek's eldest son was born after Bertha's move to the convent, leaving no alternate relationship to exclude him.

While we can rule out Grabow and Lawrence, there is nothing to say that it was or was not Karnebeek who broke Bertha's heart and forced her to the nunnery. With that said, all information related to Karnebeek is in Dutch, so something could have been missed!

Mary Austen Barber: A Married Episcopalian Catholic Nun?

Mary Austen Barber was the wife of an Episcopalian minister who was flirting with Catholicism. The minister had read the story of Saint Francis Xavier and found it so compelling that he began to question his own Protestant faith. After bearing four girls, the couple's fifth child was a boy. After his birth, the boy remained nameless because the father wanted to name him Francis Xavier but the mother refused such a popish name. It would be a few days before Mary Austen named him Samuel.

While residing in New York, Mr. Barber was asked to resign his position in the Episcopal Church after he and his wife decided Catholicism to be their true faith. They opened a small school to support their family, but the Catholic community there did not give it much thought. The one exception was Father Fenwick, who took an interest in their new devotion.

When Father Fenwick was brought to the Georgetown Visitation Convent as the new rector of the college, he continued his support of the Barber family. Through much self-reflection and discussion with each other, Mr. and Mrs. Barber decided to answer their new calling in life. Mr. Barber would travel to Rome to enter his noviciate for the priesthood, while Mrs. Barber would enter the convent.

She took the veil as Sister Mary Austen. The young Samuel and the youngest daughter were adopted into the care of Father Fenwick's mother. The three older girls were pensioners in the convent. The family continued in the care of the Visitation Convent. All four daughters became nuns and the young son a Jesuit priest.

ANN WIGHT: THE RUNAWAY NUN

Virginia Scott, Bertha Gerolt and Mary Austen Barber owed their investment in the Georgetown Convent of Visitation to love. One sought solace within its walls from a broken heart, one honored a lover's vow and the other joined with the encouragement and love of her family. Ann Wight was already a nun when her scandal began to circle throughout the town.

Sister Gertrude, the name given to Ann Wight upon taking her vows, was deeply involved in the convent. She had grown up there since the age of eleven under the care and education of the nuns. Sister Gertrude had a keen intellect and brazen curiosity that had little outlet in the cloistered walls of a religious order. When she was appointed directress of the convent's school, she was able to devote herself both to God and literature. Now with an avenue to develop her desire for devotion, Sister Gertrude was one of the most able members of the convent and highly respected by the sisters—that is until she became close with an esteemed woman of great piety residing in the convent. Madame Iturbide, the former empress of Mexico, was staying at the order's academy with her four daughters. She had brought with her a personal chaplain who was asked to act as spiritual advisor in the absence of the convent's director, who was away in Europe.

During the director's absence, Sister Gertrude, the visiting chaplain and ex-empress conspired together to usurp the entire convent. At some time in earlier years, there was an effort to rededicate the convent's cause from the order of Visitation to the Ursuline order. This was never fully realized, but the aspiration never left Sister Gertrude's mind. With the director gone, the three conspirators were able to convene with the remaining community in order to propose the change.

An Ursuline order would be better suited to the needs of Georgetown, argued Sister Gertrude. The convent was originally founded as a contemplative mission only. With the convent's repurposed dedication to intellectual studies under the new order, the academy would take a more prominent role, and with it, Sister Gertrude.

In the Father's absence, the other nuns were aghast at the attempts to subjugate the order's historic mission. They rejected the idea outright, and the discussion was abandoned. A year later, a Father from the Jesuit College, already familiar with the nuns, came barrelling into the convent. "Have you seen Sister Gertrude? Is she here?" he asked. Every room and corner was searched, but she was gone. That same Father had seen her on the street just before. He could not have been mistaken, because Sister Gertrude faced him and barred open her costumed cloak to reveal her silver cross. It was only the hope that he was mistaken that had him inquire at the convent.

In the afternoon hours, Sister Gertrude had taken the key from a student at the academy and a young girl's cloak. With a turn of the lock, she walked out the convent doors for the first time in sixteen years. Now returned to her secular name, Ann Wight called a driver to take her to the home of General Van Ness in Washington, D.C. Ann was related to his wife and stayed at his home for a time after her departure from the convent. This may have had nothing to do with the previous year's embarrassment of a failed coup. But surely some thought the sin of pride had compelled her to leave. Ann never gave a reason herself, which only fed the flames of the gossip.

Ann was remembered as a great socialite after her years in the convent. Her intellect and wit served her as a host and guest of many distinguished occasions. Her presence at these events led to whispers of an escaped nun

Mansion of General Van Ness, Sister Gertrude Wight's refuge after escaping. *Library of Congress.*

in attendance. Always ones for drama, the Georgetown and D.C. elite must have been thrilled by her story. It was an escape in the lightest of terms, as all she really did was walk out and hail a cab. In a vernacular twist, it was common to call the nuns of a convent "inmates."

During the remainder of her un-cloistered life, Ann stayed with the Van Ness family until General Van Ness died without a will, leaving her without means to survive. But Ann had powerful friends. The daughter of Madame Yturbide left Ann a share in the grievance against the Mexican government. Homeless and penniless, there was no better time to take up the cause of the ex-royal family. So Ann went to Mexico to claim her portion of what was owed. When she returned, she left for France. The former sister who was not allowed to leave the grounds of the convent had become a world traveler. When she returned to the States, the country was on the brink of civil war.

Throughout the years, Ann never talked about religion, though she continued to attend church. During the last years of her life, as she dedicated her efforts to the Southern cause, she visited the Order of Visitation in

Baltimore, where she was entreated to return to them. They wished her to die with them in the convent or return to Georgetown to die in her former home there. She refused, remarking to the Baltimore nuns how she loved to travel, and continued on her journey south to Richmond, soon to be capitol of the Confederacy. Shortly after arriving in Richmond, Ann contracted pneumonia. In her final moment, she stumbled out of bed and fell to the floor. She raised her hand to her head and said, "Oh, am I crazy?" Ann Wight quietly passed away just as she had quietly passed through the gate of the convent.

***

The Monastery of Visitation came to Georgetown as a small religious community under the direction of Archbishop Neale, who was president of Georgetown College. The community became a monastery in 1816. Ever since the school was established in 1799, it has been a center of Catholic education for women. It is likely that Virginia Scott, Bertha Gerolt, Mary Austen Barber and Ann Wight joined because of a common calling. But it was their backstories and how they discovered—or lost—that calling that proved scandalous in nineteenth-century Georgetown.

Chapter 9
Illegal Love

Prostitution on the Potomac

Writing about the history of prostitution is difficult because it was never really talked about. Everyone knew it existed but pretended it didn't. Prostitution was a necessary evil in the Civil War and a social one in the Victorian reformation of the early twentieth century. If it was mentioned, it was done so in code. Soiled doves who were no longer pure and white, gay young ducks and daughters of eve were all references to these painted jezebels. Much to the dismay of the residents of Cyprus (the home of Aphrodite, the Goddess of Love), these women may be called Cyprians, but love had little to do with their profession.

These women plied their trade on the streets, in back rooms or at established houses. But they provided more than a nightly respite from a long workday or a means to forget a bloody fought battle. We can think of them more as escorts who promenaded with their clients along the main avenues of the city. Dressed in their finest, with painted faces and feathers in their hair, they lounged in carriages, attended the theater and dined in restaurants with no concern for the whispers spoken as they passed.

When the Civil War broke out, D.C.'s population increased by 75 percent. Some of these were the madams from the large cities in the North who closed their bordellos to reopen in the Capitol. Those with the finest ladies would not open their doors in the dirty back-alley neighborhoods of the city. They wanted the fine mansions and gardens. With the money they had,

Prostitute in the street. The Days' Doings *2, June 24, 1871.*

they could afford the higher rent and nicer homes of the district's more elite neighborhoods. These brothels were furnished with the finest furniture, the cabinets filled with the best whisky and the ladies dressed in the latest and most revealing silk fashions.

At the beginning of the war, there were 450 registered brothels in D.C. A year later, there were 5,000 prostitutes in Washington City, with an additional 2,500 in Georgetown and Alexandria. More than 2,300 white and 1,200 "colored" prostitutes arrived during the war. A third were thought to be streetwalkers who were not associated with a particular house and worked where they could. This number did not include the concubines, women who lived with the lonely men of the city and sometimes even passed for their wives. This was before the end of slavery and during a time when interracial relations were not socially acceptable, even in the liberally minded capital. Some men may have kept concubines by force. Some may have treated them dearly, while others may have enjoyed their company but refused to marry someone of such standing. Either way, the increased number only counted women who were paid in cash at the end of their duty.

Just as some were entering the city, others were leaving. Even among the working girls, there was a distinct secessionist faction that remained loyal to the South. The Union may not have been aware of the Rose Greenhows and Lillie MacKalls in their midst, but it knew that southern women could cause trouble if they remained in the Union capital. Those prostitutes of the Southern persuasion were seen drunkenly singing "Bonnie Blue Flag" and praising Jefferson Davis right on the streets. Passes were issued to any woman who wished to leave with free passage to Richmond. Of the hundreds of applicants, seventy were prostitutes. These women were not prisoners, and once they reached Richmond, they were free to continue as they pleased in the Confederacy.

However, two of them were sent back. Robert Ould, a Georgetown boy, became the Confederate agent of exchange when he moved to Virginia in 1861. Two bawdy women arrived back in D.C. with a personal note from Ould. These two "strumpets" were being returned to the District. The Southern authorities assumed it was a mistake, because it would be taken as a "personal affront" if it were being done purposely. The two were released to go back to work in the city.

The ladies from the larger cities moved to the district because the money was easy. Large numbers of Union soldiers camped in and around the city, with more entering after the numerous battles in Northern Virginia. To add to the large number of potential clients, law evasion was also easy. With more than two hundred miles of streets and nearly eighty miles of back alleys, police could not be everywhere.

Despite the influx of soldiers, workers and ladies of the night, there was not an increase in the police force. The military provost acted as the city police in addition to their military duties, but they were often found in the brothels' beds themselves. A metropolitan police force was formed in 1861 with 150 men, but prostitution was still treated lightly, with small fines or a night in jail for those women who were more disorderly. The women were not forced to leave the city. When brothels were broken up, the madam paid the fines from the large stores of cash and moved on to a new house. The ladies working there were not arrested and could continue to the new location.

There were efforts to control the vice if not get rid of it completely. The area that is now Federal Triangle was known for some time as a red-light district called Hooker's Division, a play on words combining the slang for prostitute and a reference to General Joseph Hooker, who had a penchant for the ladies and was headquartered in the area. It would be easier to police if the bordellos were all in the same area. It would also be easy for Hooker and his men to "patrol." The men would go down the line and visit Fort Sumter and Headquarters USA—neither the names of military institutions though many soldiers could be found there.

As the war progressed, the police tried to shame the women off the streets. The practice during the Civil War to dishonourably discharge a soldier was to place a large placard around his neck naming and describing the details of his crime. The band would follow, playing the "Rogue's March." In 1863 in Washington, they tried to use this as means to deter crime and prostitution in the district. Two women included in the march were reported as Anna Smith and Sarah Davidson, neither showing much shame. But the embarrassment was not confined to the workingwomen. Some neighbourhoods, sick and tired of seeing horses lined up each night outside known houses of ill fame, began to keep track of who came and went in order to report them to their commanding officers and families back home.

At this point, the prosecution of prostitution and brothels was increased. Women were arrested and fined thousands of dollars. There was jail time for some. Court cases were heard instead of cast aside, as madams were no longer able to bribe the arresting officers. If there were a demand for the service, there would be a supply. In order to keep the demand low, the prosecution subpoenaed the men who frequented the brothels to testify in public about what they did and where they did it. One arrived in court wearing green goggles in hopes that no one would recognize him. The military did what it could to stop soldiers from visiting the houses. An order issued in 1862 stated that any convalesced soldier found in a house of ill fame would thus be considered fit for duty. If they were capable of participating in those acts, they were capable of rejoining the battle.

In the years after the Civil War, prostitution remained a problem in Georgetown. In 1873, Simon Dentz was charged fifty dollars for running a "disorderly house" on Greene Street. It was a known drinking establishment frequented by disreputable characters. The fine was the same five years later for Annie Wilson, who had a house on Grace Street. Wilson was given the choice to pay the fine or spend sixty days in jail—we don't know which she chose. In 1882, Robert Cooke ran a known brothel at 1058 West

Market Space in Georgetown but was only fined twenty-five dollars. The term "disorderly house" referenced a brothel, a bar or an establishment that operated as both. Many bawdy houses served alcohol in addition to women. The booze kept the men in the room and willing to open their wallets, whereas having fancy ladies in a bar kept the men coming back for more. In 1897, James Tucker was arrested for running a disorderly house in Georgetown—whether it was known for booze or broads we don't know. He was fined twenty-five dollars and three months in jail, causing him to lose custody of his three young daughters: Annie, Hattie and Nettie.

But Georgetown had an advantage in its location for the women hoping to escape the long arm of the law—the Potomac River. With jurisdictions unclear, the river provided a refuge from police in Maryland, Virginia and D.C. Should their trick be revealed, the women need only float away from their reported location. The types of boats varied, but the cheaper, easily made arks were most prevalent. These flat-bottomed boats had square ends, cedar clapboard siding and a flat tin roof painted red. They were equipped with kerosene lamps and coal-fired stoves, turning the waterway into a

The remnants of boats used as brothels at Mallow's Bay on the Potomac River. *Courtesy of Potomac Kayaking Company.*

floating red-light district. Most had one story, but others had two stories floating on the barge that housed multiple "ark girls." The larger and better-equipped arks had blue roofs and shutters to distinguish themselves.

The floating brothels could only use the waters near Georgetown in the summer. With the floods and ice flows, the arks were not safe or comfortable at other times of the year. Like the bordellos on land, there were different classes of working girls. The waters near Aqueduct Bridge in the west of Georgetown were home to less appealing women and frequented by poorer men.

With increased prosecution and a change in social acceptance of the inevitable, prostitution in the district changed. Skirts may be shorter and relations more casual today, but the visibility of noticeable prostitutes has declined. It still happens, and it's still not talked about. Surely the madams still prefer the mansions with lovely side gardens—like the ones in Georgetown—now they are just better at hiding them.

Chapter 10
Timely Traditions

Stealing the Clock Hands of Georgetown University's Healy Hall

Georgetown was its own city before becoming part of Washington, D.C. It continues to remain in many ways a separate neighborhood from the rest of the city, both socially and physically. But to many not from the D.C. area, Georgetown refers specifically to the university.

Georgetown University was founded in 1789 at the westernmost part of the city as the country's first Jesuit College. It is known for being a studious campus where students thrive in academia. High cumulative GPAs aside, it is still a college campus. As a religiously founded school, Georgetown does not have a Greek presence. There is no sorority hazing or fraternity pranks, but there remain a few traditions that dismay the administration.

The historic campus, with its stone buildings and tree-lined sidewalks, has a beautiful medieval feel about it. The most iconic building, the one that stands out as the epitomic image of Georgetown University, is Healy Hall. Designed in the Romanesque architectural style and featuring sacerdotal elements, Healy Hall in many ways reflects the religious heritage of the school. The building itself is a maze of classrooms and dormitories laid out on four floors—or five, depending on whom you ask.

Any student will tell you that there are five floors to Healy Hall. The fifth floor has been sealed off and cannot be accessed. Some say it's because it's haunted by the ghosts of slaves brought in by Jesuit priests from Maryland to work on projects around campus. Others say it's home to the ghost

Healy Hall of Georgetown University. *Author's collection.*

of a young religious student who unwisely read aloud from an ancient religious text, opening up a portal to the underworld. Without knowing how to close the portal, the school sealed up the floor to prevent students from getting in and demons from getting out. However, the university has a more practical reason—they sealed the fifth floor to prevent access to the clock tower.

The spires of Healy Hall dominate the skyline of Georgetown, the tallest being the clock tower. On the eastern and western front of the two-hundred-foot tower are clock faces with Roman numeral inlays to tell the students the time as they wander campus from class to class. The tower itself was part of the original ventilation system of the building when it was completed in the late 1880s. The clock face and three bells were added as time-keeping devices. With the bells being rung manually at the time, the paths to the tower were well and regularly traveled, but their accuracy was lacking. In the 1930s, the bells were replaced with an electronic chiming device, and those same paths grew cold and un-trodden—that is until the 1960s, when two freshmen students nicknamed KC and Scoop, as members of the infamous Holders of the Clock Klub (HOCK), found their way inside. The Holders of the Clock were nine students determined to make their way into the hallowed halls of the tower.

Picture of Georgetown University's Healy Hall with the clock missing its hands. *Courtesy of Michelle Cassidy and* The Hoya.

Through a hole in the ceiling of Riggs Library on the fourth floor, KC and Scoop entered into the forbidden fifth floor. With provisions of milk and jelly crackers and their watchmen on the other side of the locked doors, the two began to quietly pry open the boards in the ceiling of the fifth floor. This act took them four hours to complete, but then they were on their way to the clock face. The students used a hand drill to cut through the floorboards and a hack saw, wrench and screwdriver to get through the padlocked doors. On October 15, 1967, after climbing through holes, prying up floorboards, dodging other students and sneaking through locked doors, KC and Scoop replaced the clock face with a banner that read, "Tick Tock, Hock has the Clock."

The '60s were a timeless decade for Georgetown University—literally. The clock hands went missing so often that the school administration stopped replacing them so the students would be late to class and hopefully learn their lesson. After three weeks of holding the clock hands, HOCK was forced to return them. But they left their mark. On the back of the five-foot minute hand was inscribed, "Hock '71," and on the three-foot hour hand the names KC and Scoop. The students were given a forty-dollar fine and a letter mailed home as punishment.

Students who took the clock hands in the '70s thought to mail them in a self-addressed envelope to the Vatican. They hoped the clock hands would be blessed by the pope and sent back to the Catholic university. As part of the more festive Christmas tradition in the '70s, the hands were not so much stolen as redecorated. The normally dark hands were painted in red and white stripes so it seemed as if a candy cane were telling the time.

In 1989, the hands were sent a little closer to home. They were mailed down the street to the White House with a request that President Ronald Reagan personally return the clock hands to the university. Unfortunately, this request was denied, but the two hands did receive a personal escort by the Secret Service.

The clock tower theft became a tradition of sorts but was not as successful after the university increased security around the area. But tradition is an important part of the college experience, even if it is a tradition not wholeheartedly supported by the college faculty. In the fall of 2005, the hands were snatched again. Freshman Wyatt Gjullin and junior Drew Hamblen were just looking for adventure and a way to continue a tradition when they became the first clock caper of this century. The two students climbed up the building's scaffolding and through a broken window before successfully absconding with the clock hands. But the return of the goods did not go as planned, as the two were caught in the act. They were put on probation, fined $500 and had to complete hours of community service to the campus and write essays on less-dangerous college traditions.

Times had changed since the nonchalance of the 1970s, when faculty had a more "kids will be kids" approach to college pranks. Hamblen and Gjullin had merely made use of a way to get into the building with the scaffolding that the university had left behind; HOCK had actually brought tools and broken locks. The university claimed a $25,000 bill in damages to the clock face after the 2005 heist.

All the bells and whistles of the security system put in by the school administration, successively greater after each theft, still didn't thwart the tradition. At the end of the spring semester in 2012, three students identifying themselves as Goliath, Juliet and Reaper emailed *Vox Populi*, the student-run blog:

To the faculty, staff, and students of Georgetown University:

Early in the afternoon of Sunday, April 29th, 2012, Reaper, Goliath, and Juliet gained access to the restricted area above Healy Hall. After overcoming a series of countermeasures and obstacles, they entered the clock tower. In the early morning hours of April 30ᵗʰ, the crew extinguished the lights and carefully removed the hands from the eastern clock face. After the fifteen-hour operation, all three safely exited the building and removed the hands to a secure location. All may rest assured that the clock itself was not damaged in any way during the operation, and the hands are now safely en route to Vatican City to receive the blessing of Pope Benedict XVI.

Hoya Saxa!
Reaper, Goliath, and Juliet

P.S. The view from the top is truly phenomenal.

The e-mail included an attachment—a screen shot of the two clock hands lying on the floor detached from the clock face.

A few days later, another photograph and a poem were submitted to another university student site, CollegeCraig. Apparently, the hands were never mailed to the Vatican, as the students offered to return them. Tired of the publicity and wanting to ensure that they would not get in trouble, the trio offered to give back the hands, but only on one condition. In exchange for the stolen clock hands, they wanted Jack Junior, the Georgetown mascot. Jack Junior was a five-month-old bulldog pup.

The clock tower wasn't handless for long. The university officials had the remaining hands on the other clock face removed to assess damages. After $9,000 worth of repairs was complete, these hands and a replacement pair from storage (they had experienced this before, after all) were installed on the clock tower. Jack Junior remained in his post as mascot in training.

Today, the bells are still chiming, and the students crossing the campus grounds can look up to see the time. However, as of this writing, less than a year after the last Hoya heist, it's just the replacement hands on the tower. Just where are those original clock hands?

Chapter 11

The Drinks That Led to It All

Georgetown Taverns

A little-known fact about the capital of our great nation is that it was formed in a bar. But then again, so was the U.S. Marine Corps, so it's not necessarily an uncommon thing. If this fact causes you any concern, take heart in the fact that it was more of a tavern than a bar, and in the eighteenth century, taverns were a part of the civic and social scene. A tavern served beer, yes, but it also acted as a city hall, a marketplace, a banquet and dance hall, a theater box office and a library.

There were establishments in Georgetown before there was a District of Columbia, and there were establishments at the mouth of Rock Creek before there was a Georgetown. Similar to today's liquor license laws, in order to run a tavern, one had to apply for a license. This means there are a fair number of records for even the earliest of public houses

The first license was given in 1747 to Thomas Odell. But the location of Odell's Tavern and what and whom it served has been lost to history. A few years later, in 1751, Joseph Belt received his license, and the place he would eventually open became one of the most well-known taverns and ever-enduring mysteries of Georgetown.

WHERE IN THE WORLD IS SUTER'S TAVERN?

It was in Joseph Belt's King's Arm tavern that Maryland decided to establish a town in honor of someone named George. The area was becoming a bustling tobacco inspection port, and there was a ferry crossing the Potomac River. On the Virginia side of the ferry, the landowners had established a tavern to quench the thirst of weary travelers. On the Maryland side, Belt had his own. It was here that the land lots that would become Georgetown were sold.

With the town developing, Belt moved his tavern to one parcel of land at what would become Georgetown's busiest intersection. In the late 1770s and early 1780s, the tavern passed into the hands of new keepers. It was first managed by John Beall and then by Ignatius Simpson. At one point, Alexander Hamilton owned it for a day in 1776, we suspect for the purpose of protecting colonial property during the Revolutionary War. But it was the man who was in charge in 1783 that gave the tavern its most recognized name. John Suter was a Maryland farmer, and through his time as tavern keeper, he kept his farm north of Georgetown. It wasn't called Suter's Tavern officially. Its official name was Fountain Inn, but most taverns were referenced by the name of their host. Even after John passed away, it would still be known a Suter's Tavern.

The walls at Suter's Tavern witnessed the creation of a new city, destined and planned to be the capital of the United States. In 1785, George Washington stayed here during a meeting with the Potomac Company. As its president, Washington met with other members in efforts to develop the silty and tidal Potomac River into a navigable waterway. Washington's Mount Vernon home was only a few miles down the river. But if this area were to become a realistic option for the Federal City, the Potomac River needed work. The goal was to have boats that could navigate all the way out west, which at the time was Ohio. It could be done, but only if you were in a canoe or flat-bottomed boat carrying little cargo. The Potomac Company never really had federal support and never succeeded in its goals, but its members did enjoy time discussing their plans over a pint at Suter's Tavern in Georgetown.

This wouldn't be the last or most important time that Washington lodged here. After Congress agreed that the Federal City would be placed along the Potomac, Washington met with his commissioners and surveyors at Suter's. It was here that the current landowners and Washington negotiated the sale of their land to create the capital. In 1791, the landowners reached a deal, and John Suter signed the document as a witness.

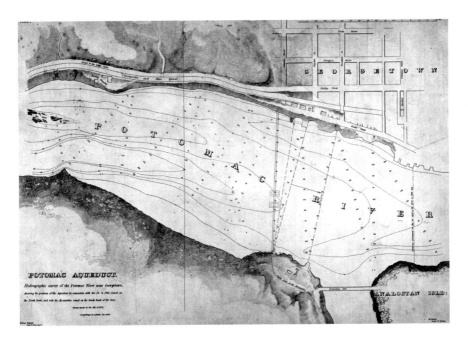

An 1832 survey of Potomac River, C&O Canal and Georgetown. *Library of Congress.*

Though Washington left to tour the country as president, the three commissioners remained headquartered at Suter's to hash out the plans for the new city. Andrew Ellicott used the tavern while he surveyed the lands, and Peter (Pierre) L'Enfant stayed here while he designed the city layout. It seems L'Enfant was a difficult man to work with and was as stereotypically French as you can get it. He made his temporary home at Suter's and kept his accounts and plans for the city and its federal buildings in his room at the tavern. While away in Philadelphia, his personal belongings were ransacked and stolen. He suspected the city commissioners, but they did not have his city plans. The culprits were never apprehended, and the theft was kept rather quiet even at the time. How Suter felt about the security of his tavern in the face of these allegations is unknown. A few years later, there was a notice in the paper that someone was stealing mail from the bar intended for those lodging at the tavern. Mr. Suter kindly asked them to stop.

With the commissioners' headquarters at Suter's, Thomas Jefferson and James Madison arrived to dine with them and discuss the plans at the behest of Washington. At this meeting, it was decided to name the Federal City. Washington City, named in honor of President George Washington, would be located in the District of Columbia. And just to confuse everyone traversing the streets of D.C., all north–south roads would be named after numbers and the east–west roads after letters. To the unwary tourist who is not aware that there are four intersections of Sixth and G—you can blame these men. After a few drinks, it was probably a very amusing idea indeed.

After John Suter's death, his wife took a few years to run the tavern herself. Their son John Jr. moved a few blocks down to manage his own tavern. By this time, Suter's Tavern had passed its prime, and the city joined together to build a much-needed new tavern. John Suter Jr. became the manager of the fledgling Union Tavern, and Fountain Inn was closed so as not to create competition. The building remained a tavern under different names and owners for the next thirty years. It even stood to witness few more important events. At the turn of the century, the tavern, now run by Francis Kearns as The Sign of the Ship, was the voting place for the Fifth District of Montgomery County during the 1800 presidential election.

In 1835, the property was sold to an unrecorded purchaser. Georgetown streets have all been renamed, some several times. In the eighteenth century, buildings did not have street numbers. Now, nearly two hundred years later, we do not know exactly where Suter's Tavern was located in Georgetown. A few claims have been proven false or unlikely. The best we can do is guess, and the best guess we have is somewhere around the intersection of M Street NW and Wisconsin Avenue NW.

THE TAVERN OF MANY NAMES

It was not always the case that the important visitors of Georgetown passed through Suter's. There were quite a few other taverns in the area. When Edmund Genet, the French ambassador to the United States in the late 1700s, made his way north from Charleston, he was intending to gain support for the French wars with Spain and Britain. A rumor after he passed through Georgetown was that he had been met with insult at Suter's. To dispel this notion, Suter put an ad in the paper stating that Genet had not even been there.

In 1796, Charles Sewell had been running the tavern at what used to be Suter's, but the building had seen better days. When a new tavern was erected on the main street, he moved there to open City Tavern. An ideal location for the civic center, it was right next to the first Bank of Columbia. The meeting room here was rented out by the Georgetown Corporation to

Rear view of City Tavern, Georgetown. *Library of Congress.*

hold its meetings, run the mayor's court and hold elections. In effect, City Tavern was City Hall.

When President John Adams came down to the newly built Washington City from the then capital of Philadelphia, he stopped in Georgetown. Adams was inspecting the buildings and area to approve the city for occupation by the federal government. The citizens of Georgetown welcomed him at City Tavern, where a banquet was held in his honor. The banquet began with seventeen patriotic toasts, to which Adams answered with a toast to Georgetown: "May it's prosperity equal the ardent enterprise of its inhabitants and the felicity of their situation."

Shortly after this visit, Joseph Semmes of the Green Tree Tavern moved in and renamed it Sign of the Indian King. Four years later, he left to run another tavern a few blocks away but then came back and renamed it Columbian Inn. Three years later, he left and took the name with him until 1822, when he came back and renamed the establishment Columbian Inn, again. Luckily, the name of taverns had little recognition in the city. Generally, taverns had signs out front for travelers. A wooden carving of an Indian king, General George Washington or a ship might indicate which tavern was at that location. But to the people of Georgetown, a place was known by its barkeep and referred to as the tavern or house of the tavern keeper.

In 1806, the Columbian Inn tavern, having been William Graham's until he left that year to run a coffee shop, ran into some legal trouble. The owner of the property, Osburn Sprigg, who had little to do with the management of the tavern, decided to sell. A plantation owner named Bailey E. Clark made the favorable proposition of a trade—plantation for tavern. Graham gave the keys to Clark once the deal was finalized. However, both owners agreed to the deal sight unseen. The plantation was not as described by Clark, and the tavern had been left open. Graham did not the lock the door when he moved so that the regulars could have access to the billiards table he left there. The court favored Sprigg and kicked Clark out.

Despite various managerial changes, the tavern continued until after the Civil War. In the 1830s, it adopted the *en vogue* French word "hotel" and became a lodging establishment. It was renamed the United States Hotel and later the Georgetown Hotel. In the 1870s, after owner Eleanor Lang failed to pay taxes month after month, Richard Morgan bought the hotel and ran it with Eleanor's grandson John Lang serving as the bartender.

As years passed, the true history behind the building was lost. The first floor was turned into a print shop in the 1960s. When it was finally discovered to be one of the oldest public houses in Georgetown, the City Tavern Club began operating a formal dining hall and private club in the building that remains to this day.

TAVERNS BACK THEN

In 1796, there were fifteen taverns in Georgetown—this is in a town that had only 2,135 inhabitants in the 1790 census. One year later, the city decided to rethink the way licenses were issued. At the time, they were issued by Montgomery County or a Dr. Beatty, both of which were indiscriminate in giving out licenses. Looking into the problem, it seemed that some were given liquor licenses without even operating a tavern. These men were now legally allowed to keep large stores of alcohol for their personal consumption.

Taverns were places that greeted presidents and founded cities. They were run by civic-minded men who were very involved in the city. Many taverns were run by women, the widows of previous owners or owners in their own right. In the early years, taverns were respectable places, but since women weren't usually involved with the running of the city business, there was no need for them to visit. But with the beginning of the women's rights movement, more women started to frequent them. There were still places, however, that true ladies did not go. One such place was a saloon located up the hill from the river in the late 1880s on what is now Wisconsin Avenue. Joe Schladt's was a place that ladies did not dare patronize. However, it did have its regular customers, and it is recorded as being a favorite spot of congressmen. Schladt's Hotel was eventually bought by William Martin.

There were also tavern owners who were not so revered by the locals. Charles Martyr ran a Georgetown tavern in the 1760s. One year, he was sued by two residents who claimed he owed them £100 for goods he bought. When they tried to collect, Martyr "removed [himself] in a secret manner from his abode." The court awarded them the £100. Having not learned his lesson, Martyr was again sued the following year. In this case, he still owed £50 of the £262 he owned for the import of goods, but he was able to get out of this suit unscathed.

Taverns during the Civil War took on a whole new role. They were used as a respite from the horrors of war, and what better way to do this than through the pint glass. It got to the point that soldiers were trading their

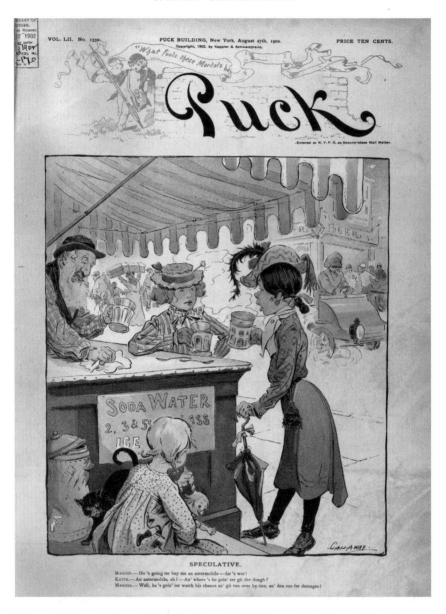

Women drinking at a bar as depicted on the cover of *Puck* magazine. *Library of Congress.*

uniforms and blankets in order to pay for their drinks. Enforcement of the illegal bars was difficult. Those that were forced shut because they had no license simply moved to a new location—much like the illicit gambling houses and brothels.

Some taverns received their closing orders for not having a license or not obeying the early closing hours. Andrew Collins ran a bar on Water Street in Georgetown and was arrested for operating on a Sunday. He had to leave twenty dollars in collateral at the station in order to be released. There was no legal recourse for closing the taverns that corrupted the young soldiers, but in 1896, there was one closed for serving the general youth. Brook Mobley and his wife, Mamie, lived in Georgetown at Market Place. Whether they actually ran a legitimate tavern or were just charged because they served alcohol is unknown. There were young boys seen drinking there frequently. One boy came so often that he became a drunkard. The Mobleys were fined twenty dollars and told there would be jail should they appear in court under the same count again.

Taverns went from a place of civic pride and meetinghouses at the turn of the century to disorderly houses during the Civil War. After World War II, taverns again turned into a place for honorable social gatherings. This time, the premiere spot in Georgetown was Martin's Tavern.

BILLY MARTIN'S TAVERN

Founded in 1933, Martin's Tavern is the longest continuously family-run tavern in D.C. today. William S. Martin emigrated from Ireland and with his son William G. Martin opened a watering hole on the corner of Wisconsin and N Street NW. The younger Martin was a star athlete at Georgetown University and eventually became a professional baseball player.

Like the taverns before it, Martin's Tavern is commonly called by the name of the owner rather than its legal business name. Luckily, it's still run by a Martin. Despite the absence of a first name on the sign, it's often called Billy Martin's, after the man who can sometimes still be found behind the bar.

During World War II, the tavern was the highlight of Georgetown's social scene. It was crowded on most nights, with the booths and bar full, and four-star generals coming in for a pint chose to sit on the floor on upturned milk crates rather than patronize another tavern. A young senator from Massachusetts could be found most Sundays with his newspaper in the rumble seat. As his love life flourished, he started to bring a young lady on dates to the restaurant famed for its secret-recipe crab cakes. He eventually worked up the courage to propose on one of these dates. Guests seated in the

Martin's Tavern. *Author's collection.*

"Proposal Booth" are treated to the history of sitting where John F. Kennedy proposed to Jackie.

The tradition at Martin's Tavern is having served every president from Harry Truman to George W. Bush. Many of them were guests before becoming president. The elder Billy Martin was good friends with Speaker of the House Sam Rayburn, and the two frequently had conversations to educate Lyndon B. Johnson. The Truman family also ate here on many occasions. In fact, Martin's is featured in one of the daughter's famous crime thrillers. And Richard Nixon enjoyed the meatloaf when he was a senator. The theory is that if you eat at Martin's enough, you might become president!

John Kerry lives just down the street at the old Bodisco house. His wife, Teresa Heinz-Kerry, frequents Martin's, usually on her own. The staff at Martin's kept telling her to bring her husband for a meal in the early 2000s. Any guesses if John Kerry ever took them up on this offer? There were probably many reasons that John Kerry did not win the 2004 election, but one of them might be that he never went to Martin's.

Billy Martin's Tavern, much like Suter's and City Tavern before it, is a Georgetown institution. The history of these establishments shows that more than just drinking occured here. Just because Georgetown declared independence from its supposed namesake does not mean it abandoned the British tradition of bonding over a pint. Where today meetings are often held over a cup of coffee, up until the mid-twentieth century, it was over a glass of beer or a shot of whiskey that one made the most important decisions. From the establishment of the town itself to the founding of Washington, D.C., from founding fathers to presidents, the taverns of Georgetown witnessed and added their fair share of history.

Chapter 12

Always at the Wrong Place

The Curse of Robert Todd Lincoln

Here's a newspaper headline you might not expect to see: "Booth Saves Lincoln." But that is exactly what happened to Robert Todd Lincoln. Robert was the eldest son of Abraham Lincoln and the only son to survive past the age of eighteen. One afternoon on a train platform in New Jersey, Robert was waiting for a train. Back then you bought a ticket from the conductor rather than at a window. It was a long line and a late night while guests were trying to buy passage south in the sleeper cars. Robert was on his way home to visit his family at the White House in Washington, D.C. On the same platform was Edwin Booth, older brother to the now infamous John Wilkes Booth. Edwin was traveling to visit friends in Richmond, Virginia. His companion for the evening was John Ford. If the Ford-Lincoln name connection seems familiar, John Ford owned a theater in Washington, D.C., in April 1865.

It is not that odd of a coincidence that Edwin Booth was traveling with the theater owner. He was an accomplished actor, much like his brother, though he was much more drawn to Shakespearean theater. He is remembered in the theater world for his role as Hamlet. The Booth family was, for the most part, thespians. The patriarch, Junius Brutus Booth, was an English stage actor named for a character in Shakespeare's *Julius Caesar*. Just to add another twist, the father Booth's namesake was Marcus Junius Brutus, the main assassin of the Roman tyrant.

Portrait of an older Robert Todd Lincoln. *Library of Congress.*

Though the date is uncertain, sometime in 1863 or 1864, Edwin Booth, John Ford and Robert Todd Lincoln were all waiting for the same train. Due to the crowds and the wait, Robert was leaning against the train. All of a sudden, the train moved. It shifted down the track only a few inches, but it was enough for Robert to lose his balance. He slipped down in the platform feet first.

He was there just a moment before his coat collar was grabbed and he was pulled back onto the platform. Edwin Booth, brother of Abraham Lincoln's assassin, had saved Lincoln's son.

Now He Belongs to the Ages: The Death of Abraham Lincoln

Robert eventually made it onto the train and down to D.C. to spend time with his family. A few years later, Edwin Booth and his brother John continued to fight their own civil war. Edwin was a Union supporter, whereas John Wilkes Booth, as we know, was an ardent secessionist. As it started to become apparent that the South was faltering, John Wilkes Booth's Southern sympathies started to take control.

It was only toward the end of the Civil War, in February 1865, that Robert joined the U.S. Army. The delay had much to do with his mother's reluctance to let him enlist. He was commissioned as a captain to serve under General Ulysses S. Grant. This was much to the pleasure of his mother, who knew he would not likely see any frontline combat in this position.

A few months later, Grant had returned back to Washington, D.C., and with him came Robert. Weary from traveling and not having slept in a real bed in weeks, he declined his parent's invitation to the theater that evening. Hours later, at Ford's Theater during a performance of *Our American Cousin*, John Wilkes Booth assassinated President Abraham Lincoln.

Asleep in his bed, Robert was awoken in the middle of the night with the news that his father had been shot. He rushed over to Peterson's Boarding House, the house across the street from Ford's Theater, where his father had been moved. In the company of his mother and members of Lincoln's cabinet, Robert Todd Lincoln was present for the death of his father at 7:22 a.m. on April 15, 1865.

This was a horrific event for a young man of only twenty-one. This was the first time that Robert Todd Lincoln was present for the death of an assassinated president, but it wouldn't be the last.

This Gun Will Look Nicer in the Museum: The Shooting of James A. Garfield

The young Lincoln had been a student at Harvard University and then Harvard Law. He never completed his studies at Harvard Law due to his enlistment in the Union army. After the tragic death of his father, the Lincoln family returned to Illinois. Robert enrolled at the Old University of Chicago to finish his law degree. After more than a decade of practicing law in Illinois, he returned to Washington in 1881 at the request of newly elected president James A. Garfield. Robert was appointed secretary of war but served with President Garfield for just four months.

At the same time that Garfield was convincing Robert Lincoln to return to D.C. as a presidential appointee, another Illinoisan man was waiting for his own political appointment. Charles Julius Guiteau never really knew what he wanted to do with his life. He continuously moved from city to city and was known for being an abusive husband. Shortly before the election of 1880, Guiteau turned to politics. His speech in favor of Garfield, titled "Garfield vs. Hancock," had a strong influence on the outcome of the vote—at least, that is what he thought. In reality, he wrote the speech in support of Grant. Once Garfield won the Republican nomination, Guiteau changed the title but not much else. He also only gave the speech a couple of times, including once on the sidewalk outside the Republic National Headquarters in New York City.

But this was enough in his mind to sway the vote in Garfield's favor and earn a political post as ambassador to Paris. So determined was he that he moved to Washington, D.C., in order to wait, or rather appeal, for this honor. He continuously wrote letters to the Secretary of State James Blaine and accosted cabinet members and Republican politicians outside the State Department and White House. In addition to the continuous annoyance of his absurd request, he only owned one set of clothes. Thus, he always arrived wearing the same outfit, often unwashed. By May, he was banned from the White House waiting room.

With no political appointment to show for all his efforts for the Republican party and President Garfield, Guiteau became determined to remove the president, this being for the good of the American people as requested by the Divine Will. Guiteau borrowed fifteen dollars from a Mr. Maynard and used the money to purchase a small pistol. He had two guns to chose from: one with a wooden handle and one with ivory. Despite the increase in price,

Guiteau elected to purchase the ivory-handled pistol, as it would look better on display—as it surely would be after he committed the act.

Having never used a firearm before, he went outside the city limits to practice his aim. Now that he had the ability to "remove the president," as he called it, he began to watch Garfield's movements. He had an opportunity and desire to shoot the president in mid-June at the train station while Garfield was sending his wife to Long Beach. Guiteau later professed that Mrs. Garfield looked in ill health at the time and he did not want to upset her more so he chose to wait until the president was alone.

On July 2, 1881, Charles Guiteau, who now owned a pistol with a showy ivory handle and was practiced enough to use it, found the opportunity to carry out his mission. President Garfield was on his way to Williams College, his alma mater, in order to give a speech. At the corner of modern-day Sixth Street and Constitution Avenue NW stood the Baltimore and Potomac train station. Guiteau had been there since morning, laying in wait and preparing for the arrival of President Garfield.

When Garfield arrived at the train station waiting room, Guiteau shot him once in the arm and once in the back at close range. Police officer Patrick Kearney arrested him immediately after the shooting. The young Kearney was so excited by the capture of the man who shot the president that he did not take the pistol away from Guiteau until they arrived at the police station. But neither Kearney nor any others seemed to be at any risk. Guiteau wanted to get caught. He had arranged a visit to the jail prior to the shooting in order to view what would surely be his living quarters. A taxicab had been arranged to wait for him at the train station and take him to the jail. Guiteau continued to claim that he was acting out the Divine Will to remove the president and was confident that the American people would come to understand that he did so for their benefit. He even wrote a letter to General Sherman telling him to bring his troops into the city and take the jail to protect him from the initial reactions of angry men before they had time to think about his actions.

In the immediate aftermath of the shooting, Garfield was taken to a more private area of the train station. Accompanying him there was Secretary of War Robert Todd Lincoln, who had witnessed the broken and shot body of his father and president just two decades earlier.

President Garfield survived the initial shootings but died on September 19. Guiteau's defense lawyers wanted him to plead insanity, but he continually asserted that he was sane. On the stand, he claimed his actions were directed to him by God and that he shot the president in order to create demand for his book, an explanation of the Bible.

Scene in the ladies' room during the attack on President Garfield. Taken from *Frank Leslie's Illustrated Newspaper*. *Library of Congress.*

Guiteau's personal defense was that he did not kill President Garfield but that the doctors had done so after the shooting. In many ways, historians believe that was an accurate assessment. Several doctors attended Garfield, and few if any washed their hands or their equipment. One of the bullets remained lost inside Garfield's body. In order to locate the bullet to extract it, Alexander Graham Bell created a metal detector to assist the doctors. Of course, neither the doctors nor Bell realized that the bed the president was lying on had metal bedsprings, which were relatively rare at the time. Without realizing the bedsprings were the cause of the detector's hits, it seemed that the bullet was everywhere—so the doctors searched everywhere.

The jury did not believe that Guiteau was insane, or at least, they did not let that convince them enough to let him live. He was declared guilty and sentenced to death by hanging. His sentence was carried out in June 1882. His last words were not a plea of innocence or dedication to the Divine Will but a poem he had written, beginning with the line "I'm going to the Lordy." His request that an orchestra accompany the poem was denied.

ANARCHY AT THE EXPO:
THE ASSASSINATION OF WILLIAM MCKINLEY

Despite the sadness that surrounded him while in D.C., Robert Lincoln remained in his post for the remainder of now President Chester Arthur's term. When the term was over, he returned to Illinois, where he continued as a lawyer and established a training school for boys. With the exception of four years serving as minister to the court of St. James in London under President Benjamin Harrison, Lincoln was content to practice law in Illinois. One of his clients was the Pullman Palace Car Company, and after the death of founder George Pullman, Robert became president of the company.

The Pullman Palace Car Company was the Georgetown mansion of train travel at the turn of the century. Not only would it have an exhibit at the Pan-American Exposition in New York in 1901, but it would also provide the presidential transportation to get there. McKinley, his cabinet, their wives and members of the press were to traverse most of the nation on the train and end the trip in Buffalo for a visit to the Expo. The April 5, 1901 issue of the *New York Times* reported:

> *The train in which President McKinley and his Cabinet will cross the continent on their travel is a marvel of luxury. It will consist of two sleeping, a dining, and a composite car, consisting of a smoking room and baggage compartment. The President will sleep in the magnificent Pullman "Olympia." A description of this car will fill an Oriental Prince with wonder. It contains five private rooms, finished in Mexican mahogany, maple, and koko. The private dining room, at one end, is furnished in Vermillion. Apartments fit for monarchs are provided for the servants.*

The Pan-American Expo was to celebrate the "progress in electrical science" thanks to the new hydroelectric power provided by Niagara Falls. Much of Buffalo and the fair were displaying the new feat of engineering, using electrically powered machines in everyday use. Through the summer of 1901, the fair would promote the advancements America had made throughout the nineteenth century.

The exposition ran from May 1 to November 2, but it would be on September 9 that President McKinley would arrive to greet guests at the Temple of Music. This would also be the day that Robert Todd Lincoln, now president of the Pullman Car Company, would arrive at the fair at the invitation of the president. And it was also the day that Leon Czolgosz came to the fair, though no invitation was extended to him personally. Czolgosz was an anarchist at a time in American history in which certain types of free speech were limited. The courts ruled that declaring yourself an anarchist in public was a breach of peace. Anarchists in Europe and America were held responsible for the deaths or destruction of royal families and government officials.

Like Guiteau before him, Czolgosz had made up his mind to kill what he believed to be an unjust president, though this time, there was no divine intervention. He may have stalked the president prior to the Pan-American Expo, but he was definitely there, revolver in hand, when the McKinleys arrived. Czolgosz decided not to make his move at the train station since the president was well guarded. On the first day touring the fair, Czolgosz was unable to get a clear shot of the president. He had one more day to find his chance.

McKinley was fond of meeting with the American public and did not enjoy a heavy security staff. At this time, despite two presidential assassinations, the Secret Service was engaged in anti-counterfeiting measures and not formally involved in presidential protection, though McKinley did have some security staff with him. The organizers of the fair believed that the Temple of Music would be an ideal location for a public reception on his last day. Czolgosz found it an ideal location as well.

Twice, McKinley's secretary, George B. Cortelyou, canceled this appearance out of fear for the president's safety. And yet twice the president rescheduled, not to be deterred in his desire to meet with the public. Robert Todd Lincoln was supposed to be at the event but was running late.

Police guarded the doors, and detectives were there to scan the grounds. Artillerymen marched along the aisle in front of the president, serving both as patriotic decorations and watchful guards. But none of the extra hands on duty did much good, as the general security rules were not being enforced. When approaching the president, hands must be open and empty, but a number of people in the crowd held handkerchiefs due to the heat, so no one noticed the man with a handkerchief wrapped around his hand approaching President McKinley. The handkerchief was concealing the revolver that Leon Czolgosz used to shoot President McKinley twice. One bullet caused only a graze as it hit a button, but the other penetrated his abdomen.

Robert Todd Lincoln had just arrived. He rushed from the train in order to get there just as McKinley met with Czolgosz. Czolgosz was captured then and there by members in the crowd and police and pummeled until

Leon Czolgosz, assassin of President McKinley, as seen in *Frank Leslie's Illustrated Newspaper*, September 9, 1901. *Library of Congress.*

the injured president ordered the beating stopped. Nine days later, he was on trial for the assassination of President McKinley. He refused to cooperate with his lawyer, and thus no witnesses for the defense were called. The court-appointed lawyer, Loran Lewis, spent more time in his closing argument preserving his reputation than defending his client. The jury deliberated for half an hour. Czolgosz was declared guilty.

After the shooting, McKinley was brought to the hospital on the fairgrounds. While it did have an operating theater, the hospital was not fully equipped to handle such a surgery. Though the fair was designed to promote the availability of electricity, it had no interior lights. Instead, a hand mirror was used to direct the last rays of sunlight onto the operating table. President McKinley died on September 14, 1901.

Though there was not enough electricity to light the operating theater clearly on the day McKinley was shot, there was enough on October 29. Czolgosz's guilty verdict was carried out by execution via the electric chair.

Robert Todd Lincoln was not by the president's side when the shooting occurred. He wasn't even in the Temple of Music yet, but he was a long way from his home in Illinois. It may have been a curse upon Robert Todd Lincoln or a set of eerie coincidences. It could also have been the fact that shortly before McKinley went to shake the hand of Czolgosz, he had given his lucky charm—a red carnation he always wore in his lapel—to a young girl in the crowd. Whether it was just a horrible case of "wrong place, wrong time," Robert was aware of the coincidences of his association with the three presidential assassinations. Needless to say, people stopped inviting him to presidential functions. He likely would not have accepted anyway. Robert's response was said to have been, "No. I'm not going, and they'd better not ask me, because there is a certain fatality about presidential functions when I am present."

Ten years later, Robert sold his home in Chicago to purchase a large brick mansion in Georgetown, the Laird-Dunlop House. Before Robert Todd Lincoln bought the house, it was owned by Judge James Dunlop. As the Southern states started to secede, Judge Dunlop held the appointment of chief justice of the circuit court of the District of Columbia, a position he held for eight years until 1863. Rumor was that Abraham Lincoln removed him from the judgeship because of Dunlop's Southern sympathies. In reality, the circuit court of the District of Columbia was abolished in 1863. No court, no judge.

So did Robert Lincoln buy the home from the heirs of a man his father kicked off the bench? Perhaps in some way, he did. Congress abolished the circuit court in an effort to reorganize the court due to questions concerning the loyalty of one of the judges. In March 1863, Congress passed 12 Stat. 762, which essentially ended the circuit court and the judgeship of the three remaining judges and created the Supreme Court of the District of

Former home of Robert Todd Lincoln on N Street NW. *Author's collection.*

Columbia. The Supreme Court had the same powers as the District Court, but the judges were different and more loyal to the Union cause.

Robert's presence in Washington did not affect the lives of the presiding presidents. However, in 1922, Robert Todd Lincoln was invited to attend the Abraham Lincoln Memorial dedication. He attended the ceremony, which was presided over by President Warren G. Harding. President Harding mysteriously died while in office on August 2, 1923, only a year and a few months after the dedication attended by Robert Todd Lincoln.

Chapter 13

The True-ish Story of the Exorcism of Roland Doe

Among the lovely homes and stately university buildings of Georgetown stands a smallish brick house set back from the road and hidden behind a large fence. There is nothing innately eerie about the house itself or the adjacent staircase between Prospect Street NW and M Street NW, but passersby always get an uneasy feeling when they walk by the "Exorcist House" and "Exorcist Stairs."

In the 1970s, *The Exorcist* was released in theaters. By today's horror-film standards and special-effect abilities, it's not completely horrifying. However, back then, tickets came with vomit bags, and theater managers kept smelling salts on hand due to the number of guests who fainted during the screenings. But there are no possessed souls or hauntings on these stairs or in this house—at least none that we know of. This was simply the set where the movie was filmed. The stairs always had an eerie feel about them. Seemingly going straight down, they were called the "Vertigo Stairs" before the '70s.

But what adds to the story is the fact that *The Exorcist* might have been based on a true story, although it didn't happen in the house on Prospect Street. In the 1940s, just north of Georgetown in Maryland, was a difficult teenage boy. There was probably one of these in most households, but the boy who became known as Roland Doe was markedly worse than most.

Roland Doe's parents sought treatment for their son. With no physical or psychological explanations for his behavior, the family turned to the

Stairs between M Street NW and Prospect Street commonly called the "Exorcist Stairs."
Author's collection.

Catholic Church. Odd things had been happening in the presence of the boy. The family reported scratching noises emanating from the walls and objects flying from table to floor without a touch from anyone.

The Catholic Church takes possessed souls and exorcisms very seriously even today. There is an International Association of Exorcists that meets twice a year in Rome, with membership restricted to those Roman Catholic priests who have their bishop's consent. These men are given psychological training to distinguish who is really in need of an exorcism as opposed to a doctor. There are a few stated signs that indicate an individual may be possessed. If one has unexplained strength, aversion to holy items, a change in personality or ability to speak an unlearned language, it may be a sign of demonic presence. Only after other medical or psychological reasons have been ruled out, and with the permission of a bishop, may an exorcism be performed. The key is patience and the ability to gain strength from within and from God.

There are express requirements and rules to performing an exorcism, and discretion is key. However, in the case of Roland Doe, the archbishop who gave permission for the exorcism to be performed also requested that a diary be kept. Its existence has allowed some public knowledge of the event. The accuracy of the diary and the press reports that followed adds the "ish" to this true story of Roland Doe. Many sources believe the stories of possession and the exorcism of this boy, but each one differs a little regarding the details of what happened, where it happened and to whom it happened.

It began in 1949 in Cottage City, Maryland—or Mount Rainier, depending on whom you choose to believe—but the two towns are not far from one another. The family was Lutheran, with a very spiritually involved grandmother and an overly protective mother. The young boy was a loner in his junior high school and like most young boys was a bit mischievous. In January of that year, the odd events started to occur. The family began to hear the sounds of scratching coming from the walls at night. Squeaking sounds were heard coming from the bed that vibrated while the boy was lying in it. Objects seemed to move on their own accord in the boy's presence. After a few nights, claw marks began to appear on the boy's body. These marks eventually manifested themselves into words.

The mother finally took her troubled son to a Catholic priest to seek the church's help. A dose of holy water and blessed candles were prescribed to the family to no avail. The lit candles were snuffed out when a comb flew across the room, knocking out the flames. At school one day, in the middle of class, the boy's desk moved across the room while he was sitting in it. This was too much for the mother to handle on her own.

Roland Doe was admitted to Georgetown University Hospital in March 1949. The story goes that he was restrained here under the advice of the same Catholic priest the family had visited in earlier months. Despite the straps that held Roland to the bed, he was able to wriggle free from the bonds and dig out a portion of metal bedspring. Using the ragged edge of the broken spring, he supposedly slashed the arm of the priest.

After only a few days here in Georgetown, the boy was taken to St. Louis, Missouri, where he had family, for further treatment. Throughout March and April, religious figures attended to him in both his family's home and the Alexian Brothers Hospital. The markings on his body continued to appear as if carved by demonic fingernails. Furniture continued to move about, and items too large to be moved by a young boy would be found on the other side the room. The boy spouted out phrases in Latin and in a vocal tone not his own. Bodily fluids of all forms were expelled in copious amounts. On a train ride back to St. Louis after a visit home in Maryland, the young Doe boy took his fist to the groin of his accompanying priest. "There's a nutcracker for you!" he yelled. Later, at the hospital, he punched a priest in the nose.

Finally, in mid-April 1949, after weeks of continuous exorcist rites, the demonic being was pushed out. Roland was free. He returned home to Maryland and re-enrolled in school. He graduated from Gonzaga High School, a private Catholic school in downtown Washington D.C. He grew up a regular family man and either has no memory or doesn't want to talk about his supposed possession.

It's a great story, one filled with the frightening images of a lost boy who cannot control his own body from the perils of a demon, his family unable to offer any sort of comfort. It's the story of a boy freed from literal hell by a strong and faithful consortium of priests. No wonder it was developed into a best-selling book and film that is still talked about as a common part of popular culture years later.

Like most Hollywood blockbusters, there was some obvious creative license with the story line and details. It seems likely that this license may have also been used by the newspaper reporters, investigators and maybe even the priests themselves. Much of what is written about the event is based on hearsay. Even the diary that is referenced in books and research is not a firsthand account. But thanks to the in-depth personal research into archives, public records and personal interviews with friends and neighbors of the "Doe" family, a little more light can be shed on this event. The author can take no credit for this painstaking research, all of which was done by Mark Opsasnik in the late 1990s as part of a series of articles written for *Strange Magazine.*

Opsasnik did not locate any hidden evidence or lost pieces of the puzzle. He simply asked questions that had not been asked before. Despite the common lore that Roland Doe lived in Mount Rainier, there is absolutely no evidence to confirm this. There is, however, plenty to place his family in Cottage City, Maryland.

The young boy in question was, by all accounts, a disturbed boy if not really possessed. Even his best friend referred to him as a mean child. Roland's father was not a central figure in this event and may not have even believed in the hype behind it all, but he let it play out nonetheless. Roland's grandmother was German and, along with his mother, was very religious. The two women may have gotten carried away with all the "old-world superstitions."

Most teenage boys had a bit of mischief about them. Roland is said to have thrived in his power over manipulating others. The friends that Opsasnik interviewed did not put much stock into the possession. Instead, they believed in a boy who took advantage of the old-world beliefs of his family. What he did with a spring bed on wheels that was easily shakable, they saw as a sign of demonic spirit. When he mimicked the priests' Latin phrases, they took it as a sign of an unnatural linguistic ability. The red welts that appeared on his body could have been a rash or even lipstick rather than the markings of a demonic spirit. No one actually witnessed most of the events used as evidence of a possession. They saw what happened afterward and heard the stories, but most of the acts were told after the fact.

We may never know the truth behind what really happened. Combining the silence of the church with the hushed nature of postwar society is a sure formula for obscuring the truth. If it were a true demonic possession, the rules of exorcisms were to keep the event secret. The family would not have wanted the information released. And if it weren't a true possession, the church and parents wouldn't want the community to know they had been duped. They would want it kept silent that the son was capable of creating such a farce. The silence of most of the involved parties just fed the flames. What is certain is that it made a damn good horror film that lent its name to what is positively the creepiest place in Georgetown.

Author's Note

I grew up always knowing I'd be the quintessential history geek. I taught high school history for about a minute, and that is all it took to realize it was not the right fit for me. I love history, and I like teaching—I just don't like grading papers, curriculum and discipline.

When my partner, Manny, and I moved to D.C., I found the perfect opportunity to teach history without all the boring bits—tour guiding. Tourists visit the monuments and memorials out of obligation, but their inner "middle-school girl" loves the gossip, rumors and scandals that surround the Capital City. The darker side of history thrills us.

Washington has its own East vs. West rivalry. As a resident of northeast D.C., there is an innate aversion to Georgetown. Sure, the buildings are quaint and the food at Billy Martin's worth the trip across town, but the sidewalks are narrow and crowded. It's inevitable that there will be a traffic jam on M Street NW and that someone with an oversized H&M bag will force you off the sidewalk and into it.

Georgetown has a great history and has had its fair share of ups and downs through poverty and prosperity—just like every other part of D.C. But the darker side of Georgetown allows it to be just that much more relatable, even to us Northeast residents.

Consider this my sordid attempt at promoting a more favorable "Eastside–Westside" relationship in Washington—my way of sharing the intriguing stories of D.C.'s oldest neighborhood and getting the tourists out of the Mall and onto the streets.

Bibliography

BBC News. "Exorcism Enters a New Age." April 27, 2000.

Conrad, Thomas Nelson. *A Confederate Spy: A Story of the Civil War*. New York: J.S. Ogilvie, 1892.

Fremont, Jessie Benton, and Pamela Herr. *The Letters of Jessie Benton Fremont*. Urbana: University of Illinois Press, 1993.

Furgurson, Ernest. "Teacher, Preacher, Soldier, Spy." Historynet.com, August 7, 2012. http://www.historynet.com/teacher-preacher-soldier-spy.htm. Originally published in *Military History Quarterly*.

Ghosts of DC. "Georgetown Canal Boatmen Brawl; Brutal Fight Ends in Murder." http://ghostsofdc.org/2012/05/31/georgetown-canal-murder-1886/.

Gouverneur, Marian. *As I Remember: Recollections of American Society During the Nineteenth Century*. New York and London: D. Appleton and Co., 1911.

Guiteau, Charles Julius, and C.J. Hayes. *A Complete History of the Trial of Guiteau, Assassin of President Garfield*. Philadelphia: Hubbard Bros., 1882.

Guiteau, Charles Julius, and John P. Gray. *The United States vs. Charles J. Guiteau*. New York: Arno Press, 1973.

Holmes, Oliver W. "The City Tavern: A Century of Georgetown History, 1796–1898." *Columbia Historical Society* 50 (1980): 1–35.

———. "The Colonial Taverns of Georgetown." *Columbia Historical Society* 51 (1951): 1–18.

———. "Suter's Tavern: Birthplace of the Federal City." *Columbia Historical Society* 49 (1973): 1–34.

Janney, Peter. *Mary's Mosaic: The CIA Conspiracy to Murder John F. Kennedy, Mary Pinchot Meyer, and Their Vision for World Peace*. New York: Skyhorse, 2012.

Johns, A. Wesley. *The Man Who Shot McKinley*. South Brunswick, NJ: A.S. Barnes, 1970.

Johnson, Jenna. "Georgetown Clock Hands Might Be Headed to Rome." *Washington Post*, May 2, 2012.

Kaplan, Sarah, and Matthew Stauss. "Healy Clock Hands Replaced." *The Hoya*, April 30, 2012.

Kelly, James. "The Spy Who Returned to the Cold." *Time*, April 18, 2005.

Kessler, Pamela. *Undercover Washington: Where Famous Spies Lived, Worked, and Loved*. Sterling, VA: Capital Books, 2005.

Lathrop, George Parsons, and Rose Hawthorne Lathrop. *A Story of Courage: Annals of the Georgetown Convent of Visitation of the Blessed Virgin Mary*. Chicago: Riverside Press, 1894.

Leech, Margaret. *Reveille in Washington, 1860–1865*. New York: Harper & Brothers, 1941.

Lescaze, Lee. "Reporter Finds FBI Eager to Make Improvements." *Washington Post*, February 4, 1980.

Lowry, Thomas P. *The Civil War Bawdy Houses of Washington, D.C.* Fredericksburg, VA: Sergeant Kirkland's, 1997.

———. *The Story the Soldiers Wouldn't Tell: Sex in the Civil War.* Mechanicsburg, PA: Stackpole Books, 1994.

Mackall, Sally Somervell. *Early Days of Washington.* Washington, D.C.: Neale Co., 1899.

New York Times. "Gen. Lawrence Divorced." March 18, 1879.

Noonan, John Thomas. *Bribes.* New York: Macmillan, 1984.

Opsasnik, Mark. "The Haunted Boy: The Inspiration for the Exorcist." *Strange Magazine* 20 (2000).

Parker, LeRoy. "The Trial of the Anarchist Murderer Czolgosz." *Yale Law Review* 11, no. 2 (1901): 80–94.

Poore, Benjamin Perley. *Perley's Reminiscences of Sixty Years in the National Metropolis.* Philadelphia: Hubbard Bros., 1886.

Qureshi, Sadaf. "Throwback Jack: Clocks and Robbers." *Georgetown Voice.* November 3, 2011.

Rosen, Ruth. *The Lost Sisterhood: Prostitution in America, 1900–1918.* Baltimore: Johns Hopkins University Press, 1982.

Smith, Tonia. "Gentlemen, You Have Played This D___D Well!" *North & South,* September 2005.

Swanson, James L. *Manhunt: The Twelve-Day Chase for Lincoln's Killer.* New York: William Morrow, 2006.

Tilp, Frederick. *This Was Potomac River.* Bladensburg, MD: Tilp, 1978.

Townsend, George. *Historical Sketches at Washington.* Hartford, CT: Jas. Betts & Co., 1877.

United States National Park Service. "The Spong Children—Chesapeake & Ohio Canal National Historical Park." http://www.nps.gov/choh/historyculture/thespongchildren.htm.

————. "Washington, D.C.—Georgetown Historic District." http://www.nps.gov/nr/travel/wash/dc15.htm.

University of Missouri–Kansas City School of Law. "The Trial of Charles Guiteau: Cross-Examination of Guiteau." http://law2.umkc.edu/faculty/projects/ftrials/guiteau/guiteautranscriptguiteaucrossx.html.

Unrau, Harlan. *Historic Resource Study: Chesapeake & Ohio Canal*. Hagerstown, MD: U.S. Department of the Interior, National Park Service, 2007.

Winkler, H. Donald. *Stealing Secrets: How a Few Daring Women Deceived Generals, Impacted Battles, and Altered the Course of the Civil War*. Naperville, IL: Cumberland House, 2010.

About the Author

Canden Schwantes is a historian and tour guide in Washington, D.C., and manages Free Tours By Foot, an international walking-tour company. When she isn't showing tourists and locals around the sites of her favorite neighborhoods, Canden volunteers at the Historical Society of Washington, D.C. With a BA from Elon University and a masters from University College London, both in history, researching (and talking about) the stories of our past continues to be a favorite pastime. Canden has a penchant for historical fiction, off-trail hiking, traveling to new locales and listening to her partner, Manny Arciniega, in any of his musical endeavors.